God and Mammon

Lloyd E. Sandelands

University Press of America,® Inc.
Lanham · Boulder · New York · Toronto · Plymouth, UK

University Press of America,® Inc.
4501 Forbes Boulevard
Suite 200
Lanham, Maryland 20706
UPA Acquisitions Department (301) 459-3366

Estover Road
Plymouth PL6 7PY
United Kingdom

Printed in the United States of America
British Library Cataloging in Publication Information Available

Library of Congress Control Number: 2009936323
ISBN: 978-0-7618-4940-7 (paperback : alk. paper)
eISBN: 978-0-7618-4941-4

Cover photo: "God and Mammon" by Keith Smith.

∞™ The paper used in this publication meets the minimum requirements of American National Standard for Information Sciences—Permanence of Paper for Printed Library Materials, ANSI Z39.48-1992

Contents

Contents

Preface

I have three aims for this book. First, I want to recognize the role business plays in establishing the moral foundations of society. Today, in many parts of the global economy, these foundations are being tested by a business culture given not to the common good but to the narrow good of business owners. A widening gulf between economics and ethics begs for a vigorous response informed by what's best in the human spirit. This places a responsibility upon business people that calls to faith for perspective:

> As men and women made in the image and likeness of God, we have been called to a responsible stewardship over all creation. Our faith in God not only provides us with a source of personal strength and integrity, but also challenges us to cooperate with the Creator in the development of a better world. Faith forms our conscience, and makes us realize that any success, in business or elsewhere, is God's free gift. As the Psalmist once put it: "Unless the Lord builds the house, those who build it labor in vain."[1]

Second, I want to say what I can about how business leaders should think about their calling. To know what ails society today we must know what it is to be human. We must begin in anthropology, with an idea of the human that can inspire and inform our lives together. For reasons I describe in detail elsewhere, I believe that this anthropology cannot be that of modern social science, which sacrifices human being to nature in ideas of evolutionary biology, psychology, sociology, and economics, but must instead be that of the Church, which raises human being to what is above nature—to the "super-natural" that is God.[2] As the chapters of this book never tire of repeating, we must come to terms with the human person. Again, from John Paul II:

> ...every social relationship, in its ethical substance, consists precisely in the recognition of the dignity of every man, in recognizing that everyone is—really—a person. If the Christian, therefore, does not let himself be guided in his social activity by this view of man, although he will be able to work out partial and technical solutions of individual problems, he will not, in the last analysis, have made society more human, but only, at most, he will have made social organizations more efficient.[3]

And third I want to take my lead from the Catholic Church, first to recognize that business is an important aspect of the "broad horizon of culture" and second to honor my Christian duty to evangelize culture by bringing attention to Jesus Christ who is the Word and the Way and who is the exemplar of the person the Creator calls us to be. Again, with John Paul II, this is the news of faith to bring to life today:

> Evangelizing culture means fostering humanity in its deepest dimensions. In order to do that, it will sometimes be necessary to illuminate with the light of the gospel all that threatens the dignity of the human person. Moreover, faith helps to produce an authentic culture because it works toward a cultural synthesis with a balanced vision, which can be achieved only in terms of the clearer light which is found in faith. Faith gives the answer from the wisdom which is "ever old and ever new," a wisdom which can help the person to adapt, on the basis of truth, the means to the end, projects to ideals, actions to moral guidelines. This will help to restore a balance of values in today's world. To put it briefly, faith, far from being an obstacle, is an effective force in the creation of culture.[4]

What follows are seven essays about the ages-old but ever new conflict between God and Mammon in business. While I wrote each to deliver its own soulful message, I also wrote each as a chapter in survey of a comprehensive ethic of business administration. The opening chapters set the stage. Chapter 1 describes the problem of being human in the challenging circumstances of business today. Chapter 2 finds answer to this problem in God, in experiences of love, play, and personhood that are too often sacrificed to Mammon, the dark lord of cupidity and greed. The middle chapters turn to the divine in business. Chapter 3 identifies the roots of the corporation in Genesis, in God's creation of Man as male and female in one flesh. Chapter 4 delineates managerial authority in God's injunction that the leader be the one who "serves the servants". And chapter 5 specifies the overarching purpose of business, not to maximize the wealth of its owners, but to honor the human person. The closing chapters bring the lessons of the book home to those who would lead in business. Chapter 6 considers the lessons that students of business must learn to fulfill God's design for our lives. And Chapter 7 celebrates the potential of business to inspire and enrich our lives by a love and beauty that calls to God. This last is not least the joyful note that business can and must strike today.

The chapters in this book are truly "essays" in that each is "an action or process of trying or testing." I began each with a question or concern. And each taught me something about business and about my faith that I did not know. Two or three brought conclusions I could not have imagined. All confirmed that the business of business is to serve our creative being in God. And all confirmed that we are in this business together:

> We are all administrators, not absolute owners, of the world that God has placed in our hands in order to make it bear fruit for the greatest benefit of all, and ultimately for His own glory.[5]

Acknowledgments

No one makes a book or anything else by themselves. I am grateful to those who've joined with me in making this book. I thank my colleagues and friends Wayne Baker, Jean Bartunek, Denny Gioia, Mary Ann Glynn, Dennis Moberg, Howie Schwartz, Gretchen Spreitzer, Kathie Sutcliffe, Jim Walsh, Monica Worline, and Amy Wrzesniewski who helped me think through a number of the book's chapters. I thank my wife Jane Dutton who, after reading a draft of the book, helped me see there were still miles to go before I could sleep. I thank those who have shared copyrights. Chapter 1 "A Thin Spot" is reproduced with kind permission from *Business and Society Review,* "A Thin Spot" (in press). Chapter 3 "Why the Center Holds" is reproduced with kind permission from *Catholic Social Science Review*, "Why the center holds: On the nuptial foundations of the corporation" (in press). Chapter 4 "Thy Will Be Done" is reproduced with kind permission from *Journal of Management Inquiry*, "Thy Will Be Done?" v. 17, 2008, pp. 137-142. Chapter 5 "Business and the Human Person" is reproduced with kind permission from Springer Science & business Media: *Journal of Business Ethics,* "The Business of Business is the Human Person: Lessons of the Catholic Social Tradition," v. 85, 2009, pp. 93-101. And Chapter 6 "Christmas Thoughts about Business Education" is reproduced with kind permission from *LOGOS: The Journal of Catholic Thought and Culture,* "Christmas Thoughts about Business Education," v. 11, 2008, pp.126-155. I thank Keith Smith whose photograph entitled "God and Mammon" graces the cover the book. I thank Paula Kopka of the University of Michigan support staff for her invaluable assistance in preparing a camera-ready copy of the book. I thank my editor Samantha Kirk and the able staff at the University Press of America. And above all, I thank God in whom we together make all things.

Chapter 1

A Thin Spot

> For naturalism, fed on recent cosmological speculations, mankind is in a position similar to that of a set of people living on a frozen lake, surrounded by cliffs over which there is no escape, yet knowing that little by little the ice is melting, and the inevitable day drawing near when the last film of it will disappear, and to be drowned ignominiously will be the human creature's portion. The merrier the skating, the warmer and more sparkling the sun by day, and the ruddier the bonfires at night, the more poignant the sadness with which one must take in the meaning of the total situation – William James[6]

And so, better than one hundred years ago, William James foresaw the danger in thinking about business today. Walled-in by natural science and directed by utilitarian values, we skate upon ice that is rapidly and dangerously thinning. This chapter is about how we think about business and about how we must think differently to keep ourselves from a sad demise.

In Word and Thought

What's in a word? There was a time when people in business were called *personnel*; today they are called *human resources*. And there was a time when the business art was called *administration*; today it's called *management*. Between these vernacular changes, from *personnel administration* to *human resources management*, the meanings of business move from the concrete (a body of persons) to the abstract (an asset of business), from the subjective (personal) to the objective (resource), and from the existential (provide or supply something necessary or helpful) to the instrumental (control a thing or person). Talk about business today is harder, more determined, and less sympathetic.

The meanings of business tell a story of the ascendance of a utilitarian science of business and with it a shift in focus and priority that Pope John Paul II identified as moving from a spiritual idea of 'work for man' to a secular idea of 'man for work'.[7] The story began to gather in the industrial revolution of the 19th century with applications of time and motion study to industrial production.

The story continued in the 20th century with the extension of rational methods of optimization to virtually all forms of business activity, including service, sales, marketing, logistics, accounting, finance, decision-making, staff support, research and development, and management itself. Today, there is hardly a part of business untouched by such rational methods and few businesses succeed without their superior application (think only of economic giants such as Wal-Mart, Toyota, General Electric, and McDonalds's).

Frederick Taylor was among the first and most persuasive champions of this so-called "scientific management," which he saw as more than a technique, but as a guiding philosophy for business.[8] It is a philosophy epitomized by what he called the "task idea":

> Perhaps the most prominent single element in modern scientific management is the task idea. The work of every workman is fully planned out by the management at least one day in advance, and each man receives in most cases complete written instructions, describing in detail the task which he is to accomplish, as well as the means to be used in the doing the work. And the work planned in advance in this way constitutes a task which is to be solved, as explained above, not by the workman alone, but in almost all cases by the joint effort of the workman and the management. This task specifies not only what is to be done, but how it is to be done and the exact time allowed for doing it.[9]

Scientific management sees the worker, not as a person to be ministered to, but as a resource to be managed. The worker is not a being in body, mind, and spirit, but a collection of movements to sequence and optimize. Scientific management divides mind from body by subjecting the doings of the worker to the thinking of the manager.[10]

To be sure, a philosophy as neglectful of the human person as scientific management could not but invite dissent. And such there has always been; at times timid, at times outraged, but never effective. It was there even at the outset. For example, in an otherwise hard-headed manual about industrial enterprise, Edward Jones could still say this about the "art" of business administration:

> Administration is chiefly a task of handling men. Its methods must conform to human nature. It should educate and interest men, and so conserve the delicate tissues of mind and body from which all human energy proceeds, that disease, premature invalidism, apathy, antagonism, and all other negative and destructive factors shall be reduced to the lowest possible sum ... Modern industry is often too prosaic and too mechanical to arouse men. ... The new day in administration will see a way found to introduce into industry more spice and romance, and more exercise for the emotional nature,--more strategic play to capture the interest, and more fine, imaginatively presented aims to awaken real devotion.[11]

By the mid 20th century, as scientific management colonized more and more of industrial life, concerns about its humane limits turned into alarms about its costs to the person and to society. Drawing from the cautionary sociology of Frederick Le Play and Emile Durkheim, Elton Mayo worried that the large changes in the techniques of industrial organization had not been met by commensurate improvements in techniques of harmonious collaboration.[12] The social aspects of "progress," Mayo warned, were being ignored at great peril. Chris Argyris complained that industrial management turns adult workers into children, and thereby stunts their full and rightful development of personality.[13] And, taking the view of managers, Douglas McGregor importuned for the "human side of enterprise" in hopes the dismal assumptions of rational management (what he called Theory X, which assumes that workers dislike and avoid work, want for ambition, avoid responsibility, and must be "coerced, controlled, directed, and threatened with punishment," p. 34), could be overturned by enlightened assumptions of adaptive integration (what he called Theory Y, which assumes that workers seek work as eagerly as they seek play, direct themselves willingly toward organization ends, and exercise a "high degree of imagination, ingenuity, and creativity," p. 48).[14] But even in chorus, these mid-century voices could only shout into the wind of historic inevitability. Their calls for reform in human relations, humanistic management, and Theory Y integration of person and organization did not have the grip or strength to uproot an idea that had sunk so deep and reached so far.

In the ambiguous perspective of near history, the current era in management thinking seems to have begun in the last gasps of the old. In 1982, Thomas Peters and Robert Waterman sought the grounds of business excellence in a best-selling book of nearly that title.[15] Viewed in retrospect that book now seems to be a watershed, a ridge that divides the humanism of the past from the "financialism" of the present.[16] That book focused on the now quaint idea that business success comes by "productivity through people". Peters and Waterman implored managers to remember what used to be axiomatic—that the good of a company rests with those who do the work. The key to managing people, they argued, is to give employees what they most want and need in this life; "meaning."

In their call to meaning, Peters and Waterman drew upon the writings of cultural anthropologist Ernest Becker, whom they quote approvingly (and to whom we will return):

> Society ...is a vehicle for earthly heroism...Man transcends death by finding meaning for his life ... It is the burning desire for the creature to count. ... What man really fears is not so much extinction, but extinction with *insignificance* ... Ritual is the technique for giving life. His sense of self-worth is constituted symbolically, his cherished narcissism feeds on symbols, on an abstract idea of his own worth. [Man's] natural yearning can be fed limitlessly in the domain of symbols. ... *Men fashion un-freedom* [a large measure of conformity] *as a bribe for self-perpetuation.* [17]

Thus Peters and Waterman supposed that "men willingly shackle themselves to the nine-to-five if only the cause is perceived to be in some sense great" (p. xxi). Excellent companies, they concluded, provide such meaning for their people:

> For example, the manager of a 100-person sales branch rented the Meadowlands Stadium (New Jersey) for the evening. After work, his salesmen ran onto the stadium's field through the players' tunnel. As each emerged, the electronic scoreboard beamed his name to the assembled crowd. Executives from corporate headquarters, employees from other offices, and family and friends were present, cheering loudly.[18]

Unfortunately, in their zeal to identify heroic corporate culture as the fount of meaning and the ground for financial success, Peters and Waterman failed to take the full measure of Becker's theory of earthly heroics. Becker also recognized that such heroics are self-contradicting and self-defeating[19]. There is an obstacle to meaning that the person cannot overcome—namely, to admit what he/she is doing to earn his/her self-esteem. Becker wondered what becomes of meaning when a person realizes that his/her society's system of "earthly heroics" is culturally-specific and thus arbitrary, and is historically-contingent and thus ephemeral. How could such meaning be a defense against extinction? Becker did not answer this question (a question he called "the main psychoanalytic problem of life") and neither do Peters and Waterman. But it is *the question.*

Today, aside from a few university academics, there are few to write about the human dimensions of work, about what work has become, about what it feels like to work, or about whether work contributes to the well-being of person or society. [20] The action in business thinking has moved from Main Street to Wall Street, from prosaic details of workaday labor to glamorous intrigues of finance. As journalist Michael Kinsley has observed:

> Modern capitalism has two parts: there's business and there's finance. Business is renting you a car at the airport. Finance is something else. More and more of the news labeled "business" these days is actually about finance, and much of it is mystifying. Even if you understand—just barely—how it works, you still wonder what the point is and why people who do it need to get paid so much.[21]

Today's indifference to the mundane humane has perhaps many parents; among them a growing wage disparity that divides the lives of managers and workers, a booster-ism for the ersatz humanism of corporate culture that trades hollow heroism for human being, a cultural thrall to CEO celebrity that expands managerial prerogatives and selfishness, a resignation of managers to global competition that demands productive efficiency before quality of work life, but most of all a new financialism that puts the welfare of business owners (often public stockholders) before that of business employees. As noted by Kingsley, business today is about managers making money for stockholders, not about managers making humane lives for employees. Today, a generation removed from Peters and Waterman, the worker more and more enters the business equation as an asset to be deployed like any other, with an eye to return on investment.

Thus the history of thinking about business is one of an opportunistic and ever more thorough rationalization of the business enterprise. It is a story of putting capital, including human capital, to the utilitarian end of making a profit. And, as we are about to see, it is a story about the demise of our human person. It is a story of thinning ice; of an idea of ourselves that looks more solid than it is and that grows more treacherous by the day.

Being at Odds

At risk in business thinking is our very being, our human person. What is this person? Is it to know by outer appearances, by its material presence and effects on the world? Or, is it to know by its inner being, by what it *is*? Between these ideas we are today torn; one of the person as a natural object that we can see and talk about (this is the idea of science, the idea of *human nature*); the other of the person as an inner spirit or 'soul' that we can know but cannot see and cannot talk about so easily (this is the idea of religious faith, the idea of *human being*).[22] Much as we might like to refuse the distinction between the two—to suppose simply that the person is the object in nature that science describes—we know better—that the person is also a spirit or soul beyond nature that faith describes. Our thinking about the human person, about ourselves, thus presents an antinomy; an apparent contradiction between outer and inner existences, both true.

And so we find the person in thinking about business today—an inner being or 'soul' at odds with the outer world of things and events. The trouble in business thinking begins with its scientific objectivity, and particularly with its basic idea that business is a rational deployment of capital assets and resources. To be sure, as its boosters are quick to point out, this powerful idea has yielded a rich harvest; a work-life substantially eased by machinery, a standard of living enhanced by increases in productivity, a new age of medicines and better health, and a culture enriched by new modes of expression and new means of communication. According to economists Milton and Rose Friedman, these and myriad other economic wonders are the determined result of the (ideally free) play of physical and human capital: "... the two have reinforced one another. The physical capital enabled people to be far more productive by providing them with the tools to work with. And the capacity of people to invent new forms of physical capital, to learn how to use and get the most out of physical capital on a larger and larger scale enabled the physical capital to be more productive."[23]

But at the same time, this powerful idea has come at the expense of the human person who is reckoned as but an economic "asset" or "resource" to be deployed like any other. According to Pope John Paul II, this idea of the person cannot be justified or sustained: "A business cannot be considered only as a 'society of capital goods'; it is also a 'society of persons' in which people participate in different ways and with specific responsibilities, whether they supply the necessary capital for the company's activities or take part in such activities through their labor."[24] Business activity, the Pope argues, must be checked by "a strong juridical framework which places it at the service of human freedom in its totality."[25]

Scientific thinking about business errs in seeing human persons as objects—e.g., as "capital" or as "workers" or as "factors of production." This is an error of perception that psychologist Owen Barfield found to be typical of the human sciences and which he identified as "failing to save the appearances."[26] According to Barfield, the human sciences too often fail to remember that what they objectively observe (what philosopher Immanuel Kant called 'phenomena') is but an appearance of what is actually true (what Kant called 'noumena'). Asking whether the sciences do justice to human life, bio-ethicist Leon Kass finds a disjunction between the vibrant living world we inhabit and enjoy as human beings, and the limited, artificial, lifeless, objectified re-presentation of that world we learn from science.[27] Scientific abstraction, he notes, is morbid. It *homogenizes* human life by overlooking its particulars of form and activity, *shreds* human life by mistaking its parts for the whole, *diminishes* human life by turning its essences (of language, passion, wakefulness, imagination, and suffering) into matter in motion, and *falsifies* human life by denying its freedom in non-teleological causal explanations. Such are the dangers that led existentialist philosopher Soren Kierkegaard to complain of science that its method: "...becomes especially dangerous and pernicious when it encroaches on the realm of the spirit." "Let science deal with plants, and animals and stars;" he continued, "but to deal in that way with the human spirit is blasphemy."[28] Lost in the objectifications of scientific thinking about business is the human person.

Darkening the shadow cast on business thinking by scientific objectivity is the shadow cast by the utilitarian precept that business is an instrumentality; that is, a means to an end. Again, to be sure, there is no denying the value in business of using resources wisely to pursue worthwhile ends.[29] And indeed, the benefits of business planning, logistics, statistical process control, and management by objectives are too obvious and well-known to need recounting here. But, at the same time, as in the case of scientific objectivity, an emphasis on ends or purposes becomes a danger when these are pursued at the expense of human life and spirit. "That which we call purpose," observed Catholic theologian Romano Guardini:

> ...is the distributive, organizing principle which subordinates actions or objects to other actions or objects, so that the one is directed towards the other, and one

> exists for the sake of the other. That which is subordinate, the means, is only significant in so far as it is capable of serving that which is superior, the end. The purpose does not infuse a spiritual value into its medium; it uses it as a passage to something else, a thoroughfare merely; aim and fulcrum alike reside in the former.[30]

Thus, when seen only from the standpoint of purpose, the human person in business does not have intrinsic value (he/she does not exist in him/herself), but only extrinsic value (he/she exists for something else). Indeed, this logical property of purpose points to a paradox of economic science; namely, that its supposition of an all-encompassing purpose of 'self-interest' denies the inner being of the self to which it refers. By the logic of economics a person exists not in him/herself but for his/her self-interest. Thus while economics presents itself as the human science *par excellence,*[31] its humanism is empty and contradicted. Its 'self-interest' refers to no recognizably human self—its economic actor has no unique personality, no individual tendencies, and no scruples written upon the heart; in a word, no inner being. And its 'self-interest' refers no recognizably human interest—its economic actor's choices are not freely elected but are dictated by the rational imperative to maximize utility (or, in psychological variations of the theory, 'expected utility'). The 'person' of economic science is not human, but is a conduit or instrument of objective circumstances; he/she is a cipher.[32]

By now the reader might well ask why these two aspects of business thinking—of scientific objectivity and purpose—that have been a focus for so long (since the industrial revolution at least) should bulk large today. Why should inner being—human being—be especially at risk now? The answer is to find in the sort of catastrophe that is occasioned by small changes that accumulate and ramify over long periods of time. All of a sudden the world is changed. The catastrophe of business thinking—the thin spot on which we skate today—is a consequence of two tendencies that have, unfortunately, reinforced one another. As today's emphases upon objectivity and purpose in business have waxed, the original religious emphases in business have waned.[33] The one has come at the expense of the other. As sociologist Max Weber showed, business thinking in the new world of America got its start and its early license in a Protestant Christianity that saw gainful work and saving as signs of election by God; ideas Weber identified with the spirit of capitalist enterprise.[34] If this Christian heritage seems an improbability to us today perhaps it is because it is so layered-over by the objectivity and purpose of modern business thinking. The old Protestant work ethic—which saw business as being for the spiritual dignity of the person and community—has given way to a "success ethic"—which sees business as being for the wealth of its owners.[35]

Although it must remain for another day to catalogue the events that brought this epochal change in business thinking, two bear brief mention. One is that capitalism's success in generating wealth not only encourages, but demands for its continued success, indulgence in worldly goods at the expense of humane goods. As described long ago by writer and critic Marya Mannes, the result has been a loss of inner being to a marketplace that asks of nearly everything, "*But, will it sell?*"

> There is just so much inner space in each man, and what fills it is the measure of the man; the extent to which, beyond the daily concerns, he can address himself to the grand questions of life and death, of love and creation. If this miraculous inner space becomes—through cumulative and incessant exposure to what is trivial, superfluous, and irrelevant—as cluttered as the aisles of the supermarket, it ends by losing its primary function as the sanctuary of conscience and the seat of thought. The man who is a victim of things is neither free nor excellent. Living more and more by the priorities of possessions, position, and purse, he does not see beyond them.[36]

Today, this event is cast less sensitively as a totalitarian consumerism that corrupts children, infantilizes adults, and destroys citizenship.[37] According to economist Thomas Frank, what has happened is worse than a distortion of inner being; it is an inversion of the truth.[38] For today's "market populists" the market is not an impersonal mechanism of exchange, but its opposite, a loving mother who takes care of her children's every need:

> The market, if we would only let it into our hearts and our workplaces, would look after us; would see that we were paid what we deserved; would give us kind-hearted bosses who listened, who recycled, who cared; would bring a democratic revolution to industry that we could only begin to imagine.[39]

To this way of thinking, the market can only be good; indeed it is the arbiter of all that is good. To this way of thinking, there is no place for a person's inner being; no place for an inner truth apart from the outer truth of the market.

A second event behind our condition today, one that predates and is in many ways responsible for the first, has been the business-abetting philosophy of pragmatism promulgated in the 19th century by the same William James that has given this essay its metaphor of thinning ice. According to pragmatism, the truth of an idea or practice lies not in any rational ideal or religious absolute, but in the practical difference it makes to act as if it is true.[40] It is a philosophy James identified with business. The truth of an idea or practice, he wrote, is its "cash value;" its value for the purpose or program at hand.[41] Despite its modesty about truth and its even-handed concern for 'differences that make a difference', pragmatism has proven to be a dangerous idea. To judge a thing by our purposes is to set aside its inner virtue for the virtue we find in it. In a word, it is to make ourselves gods of the good. To twist a phrase of Hollywood movie, it is to make our greed good. One can only wonder what James would think to see how far this idea has been taken—to see that it is nearly an axiom today that the truth and good of a business idea or practice is the profit in it. One hopes that he'd be chagrinned, that he did not intend to set this bonfire upon the ice we today skate.

A Being Not Our Own

As we've seen, business thinking today skates upon a thin spot of its own making; namely that of our inner being—of our human being. It is a bargain of outer plenty for inner poverty. As we've also seen, in connection with Ernest Becker, the problem of inner being is rooted in the problem of meaning. To exist in and of oneself is not to be an object of science or an instrument of purpose, but to have meaning unto oneself. Only a self which exists beyond objectivity and purpose, in the strictest senses of these words, has its own meaning. The inner poverty of business thinking today is just that of its lack of personal meaning. It gives no place to the human person.

Recognizing this alliance between meaning and being, writer Walker Percy sought understanding of the latter in studies of the former, particularly in the writings of philosopher Charles Pierce on semiotics.[42] According to Percy (and Pierce), meaning is created in the social act of *naming* by which people join their common experiences under a shared symbol. Naming gives meaning to an experience by establishing that it is *about* something. This *something* is its meaning. The act of naming is truly a wonder; by its power we not only bring meaning into being, we also bring ourselves into being, both in a godlike *creatio ex nihilo* (creation from nothing). As Percy points out, unlike all other animals, which live as 'organisms' in an objective 'environment,' we live as 'beings' in a meaningful 'world' that we ourselves create.

The act of naming is as ordinary as a father who pairs the sound "ball" with the round object he puts in his son's hands. As the round object is named it comes into being as a meaning—it becomes an abstract idea or concept of "ball" in the human "world." And at the same time, as the round object is named the father and son themselves gain a measure of meaning and being—they come to be in a "world" that includes such things as "balls." But for its ordinariness, the act of naming is not the less mysterious. Hidden within it is a cataclysm that separates the father and child from every other kind of creature on earth. The father may pair the same sound with the same ball for his golden retriever, but to a dramatically different effect. For the dog, the sound "ball" is never more or less than a command to find and return a particular thing, which invariably he bolts off to do, tail wagging. For the dog, "ball" is a physical stimulus that evokes a physical response. But for the child, there comes early a realization that the sound "ball" refers not only to a particular round thing, but as well to an abstract class of round things, which by further acts of naming he will understand in detail—for example, that the round things in the box of sporting equipment in the garage are "balls," but that the big round thing on dad's desk is a "globe" (and not to be tossed), and that the little round thing on mom's dresser is a "bottle of perfume" (again, not to be tossed). All of this, so familiar to human experience, is lost entirely on the dog.[43]

Would that our human story was one of naming alone; that in this ordinary act we had answers to all questions about the meaning of our lives and about our human being. But in what has to be humankind's great comeuppance, the blessings of naming come with a monstrous curse. Our fate is to be able to name every thing in creation (Biblically, all of creation, "the fish of the sea, the birds of the air, the cattle and all the wild animals of the earth, and every creeping thing that creeps upon the earth") except one—the most important one—our own self. As Percy describes so humorously and well, each of us looks outward from the center of our own personal cosmos and, together with others who look outward from the center of their personal cosmos, name and bring into being all that comprises our "human world."[44] But from this position looking out at the world with others the one thing we cannot name and cannot bring into being is our self and this for the simple reason that it is not outside for all to see but is inside at the center of our cosmos. In search of self we look out onto the world to seek meaning and being in the things we can see and name, not least the things of business, science, art, liturgy, sport, and whatever. It is, however, a futile and despairing search. To look for self in outside things is to not find it. It is to be, in Percy's choice words, "lost in the cosmos." Thus our self—our inner being—is an unsolvable a mystery—indeed, *the mystery*. Somehow, and with philosopher Rene Descartes, we know *that* we are (in his formulation, "I think therefore I am"), but not *who* we are.

What then is this inner being that we cannot name and that business thinking keeps from view by its unforthcoming occupations with objectivity and purpose? What is the meaning of self? And what is it to be a person? We come to a perhaps surprising answer if we hold to the semiotic principle that meaning and being consist in a social act of naming. If, as we have seen, we cannot name the self with others because we and they we are marooned at the center of different cosmos', then we can name the self only with one who shares our inner being, with one who knows us at least as well as we know ourselves. And here, at last, we come to the possibility suggested earlier by the antimony between our nature and spirit, between what we can know of self by science (human nature) and what we can know of self by faith (human being). Here we come to reason joined by faith. By the light of most faiths, and certainly of the author's own Roman Catholic faith, we are named and brought into being by God, the Father who pairs the word "I" with the life He puts in our hands. We come to be and come to know who we are in relation to the God who knows everything about us and who has made a place for us in His kingdom. In God, and only in God, we have a true name, a true meaning, and a true being. In God, we are someone, a self.

Given this truth of faith, that our human being lies not in the "world" that we have made but in God, we can better appreciate the thin ice on which business thinking today skates. In particular we can better see the dangers that come of thinking about ourselves in its remote and alienating terms of worldly objects and purposes. An obvious danger is the empty consolation of consumerism noted above; of taking comfort in the prosperity of business and the beneficence of the market. A second danger, less obvious perhaps, is the false hope of diversion; that the alienation of business thinking can be allayed or placated in ordinary ways, such as by taking a vacation, or going fishing, or having the grandkids over for cake and ice cream. But, and precisely because such diversions can be joyful, such escapes take us farther from self, as philosopher Blaise Pascal saw long ago:

> The only thing which consoles us for our miseries is diversion, and yet this is the greatest of our miseries. For it is this which principally hinders us from reflecting upon ourselves, and which makes us insensibly ruin ourselves. Without this we should be in a state of weariness, and this weariness would spur us to seek a more solid means of escaping from it. But diversion amuses us, and leads us unconsciously to death.[45]

A third and most serious danger is the supposition that we can create our own meaning and being. This last is the reckless mistake we make today in thinking about business. Again, we have been given the great power of language to name and thus bring into being everything in the world, except ourselves. But we abuse this power to think of ourselves not in the terms God has set for us (He who made us in His image and who revealed Himself to us in scripture and sacred tradition), but in the suicidal terms of objectivity and purpose we set for ourselves. Instead of looking for the meaning and being of our lives where we must—to God—we look where we can—to the objects and purposes of business or to other aspects of the world we have made for ourselves. In making this mistake—a mistake first made by Adam and Eve in the story of Genesis and a mistake we repeat endlessly in legacy of their "original sin"—we are reminded of the wisdom of Saint Paul who in *Romans (12:2)* advises: "...be not conformed to this world: but be you transformed by the renewing of your mind, that you may prove what is that good, and acceptable, and perfect, will of God."

He Will Be Served

In recounting how business thinking has come to a harder, more determined, and less sympathetic idea of the human person, we noted the antinomy between our nature (as an object in the world) and our being (as a spirit or soul). We saw how, by denying the food of faith that acknowledges inner being in God, business thinking gobbles a poisoned reason focused on outer objects and purposes. This would be a grim and sad story indeed if this were its end.

But it is not. There is always saving grace. We cannot misunderstand and mistreat ourselves for long. However we may stifle and deny our human being, it demands to be served as God demands to be served—and this because it is God in us. Business thinking need not be a soulless exploitation of human capital at the expense of the human person. It can and must be a celebration of the human person in all of his/her spiritual dimension, even while it pursues a necessary and healthy profit.[46] That we cannot deny God in our lives is a truth written on the human heart, a truth that however we may try to hedge or refuse we cannot help but know.[47] On the broad scale of whole societies this is to see in the inevitable failures of communist or fascist tyrannies that try to keep people from God by putting the state in His place. This is to see no less in the inevitable failures of capitalist economies that try to keep people from God by diverting them in consumerism.[48] On the narrow scale of our individual person this is to see in the inevitable pangs of conscience that we feel when we try in myriad ways to put our own idea of self before God. The grace which funds our resilience is our sure sense and constant hope of human being which comes as a gift from God. In our freedom we may leave the gift unopened or forgotten, but we cannot destroy it, not even by sin. The God who created us in His image wants us to live in His image.

At chapter's end we return to its beginning, to the wisdom in words. We asked what has been gained and lost in our historical transit from personnel administration to human resources management. We see that gains in productivity and wealth have come at the cost of impoverished being. Whereas we think of ourselves as *human resources*, as corporate assets put to profit, in God we can think of ourselves as *persons* of intrinsic dignity and worth. And in this latter divine word, at the root of the word personnel, we have a being to hold onto and to cherish. And whereas we see business as *management*, as a manipulation of means for ends (the image is of trainer and horse, or more darkly of master and slave), in God we can see business as *administration*, as a ministry by those who lead to provide for the whole person of those who follow (the image is of a servant king, or of a good shepherd). While it may be hard to imagine taking these words back in business today, it is harder still to imagine embracing a life that is not ours, a life without being, a life without God. With these few words at least, let us edge away from the thin ice of a human being worn down by the objectivity and purposes of business and instead skate with confidence upon thicker sturdier ice of a human being in God.

Chapter 2

Being at Work

"Who am I?" It is the ageless question I share with all. It is the question of my life, whether I live it well. It is the question of my work, whether it is worth the while. And though I ask it again and again, it is the question whose answer I forget again and again. And for this, I suffer.

"Who am I?" is truly a question, for its answer is beyond my reach. As a person I live, not as an animal, not as an organism in an environment, but as a being in a *world* of meaning that I make with others.[49] And although this being or "self" is a phenomenon *in* nature, it is not a phenomenon *of* nature. It does not have natural causes, it is not a result of evolution; it is beyond such things. It is the mystery of human being. And truly it is a mystery, for while I can know the name and place of every thing in the world, I cannot know the name and place of my self. I am not big enough to take myself in. I cannot know the knower. From my spot at the center of my world I look in all directions and see every thing in the cosmos but my self. I am, strange to say, lost at the center of the cosmos.[50]

In Search of Being

Being lost is no place to be. Somehow, somewhere, I must find out who I am and how I am to live. I must find the ground of my being and my power to act, to love, and to live. I must find my self, at work and everywhere else.

Being a man of the now post-modern age, I might look for my self in science, the religion of the age, the authority of authorities. But I would be disappointed; for two reasons at least. First, science deals in abstractions. It describes the self, not in its particularity, but as it can be boxed by generalities of personality and culture. My self—that which is not categorical and which distinguishes me from others—is precisely what science cannot say. Second, science builds its image of the self upon a confusion of human being and human nature. In this image I am incoherent; my elements do not "stick together". I am at once subject and object, mind and matter. I am the person of the scientist himself, a subject who defines the world and decides what he will do in it; *and* I am the person studied by the scientist, an object in time and space, an effect of complex causes.[51] I am at once disembodied freedom without ground or rule, unable to act on what I think or decide, *and* I am mindless determinism without free-will or personal agency.[52] Either way, I am not recognizably human.

Alternatively I might look for my self in faith, in what is revealed to every human heart, written in Holy Scripture, and interpreted by religions. Faith is before science, "… the knowledge which the human being has of God which perfects all that the human mind can know of the meaning of life."[53] According to faith, I am in God. In the Christian faith, I am Adam, fallen man of the Old Testament, liable to sin and destined to struggle and toil unto death, and I am Christ, redeemed man of the New Testament, pure of heart and destined for eternal life. In the persons of both I am made by God in His image as his beloved Child. According Thomas Aquinas, my essential act (my *actus essendi*) is my being in God.[54] And according to Josef Ratzinger, now Pope Benedict XVI, my person is "the event or being of relativity."[55] I am as I live in God and as I live in others in God, as "I" and "Thou."[56] I am neither the pure mind nor the mere object of scientific account; I am a moment of love in the eternal encounter of man with God.

How different I am in faith than in science. I am neither subject (mind) nor object (body), but before and more real than these scientific categories. The "I" that is my self is a unique person named and loved by God. Although not simply material, I am embodied, *here,* in time and space. And although not simply mental, I create a "world" for my self by my many and varied acts of naming. To be in God changes nothing and everything. What is not changed is that I am still alone in the cosmos, still faced with the problem of coming to be. I still have to be who I am. What is changed, and it is everything, is that I know who I am. I am a child of God. To be myself, whenever and wherever I am, I must be in God.

Work against Being

> Self-realization is a contradiction and it is too little for us. We have a higher destiny.[57]

Too often my work flies from being. Some of this cannot be helped I suppose; for the bend of my work to worldly purposes and the concern of my work for efficiency can easily divert me from God, the source of being. To wit, as I write this chapter I am aware of its purpose (to persuade you of something); I have hopes for its virtues (that it be clear and maybe even engaging); and I know it is to be judged, not least by a publisher and you dear reader. Amid these externalities—which press upon me because I want to persuade you, write a good chapter, and have you and others think well of it—I am led not to God and to being, but in the opposite direction to my ego. I take it into my head that the chapter is me. I think of its success or failure as existential. Should the chapter be persuasive, then I am persuasive. Should it be clear, efficient, and engaging, then I am likewise. Should it be popular, garner praise, and make a buck, then so much the better of me. And, alas, should the chapter be none of these things, then I am none of these things. In a word, I mistake the chapter for my self. In a deeper word, I mistake something I create (the chapter) for the thing that God creates (me). And in the deepest word, I mistake my self for God.

In this and a thousand other ways I meet my anxious question, "Who am I?" with the catastrophic answer that I am what I create, what I say, what I feel, what I do, what I have, and so on. Whereas I would do well to see what I create as testimony to the glory of God who created me, I see it instead as testimony to my ego, or rather as the substance of my ego. And in this outlook I do not think I am alone, for so much of work today seems to have similarly anxious foundations. Its many divisions of position and rank, its grades of compensation, and its underlying economics of profiteering, are contests for status and meaning. You ask: "Who am I?" "Why, I am the one who is full professor of psychology at the famous university in town, the one who writes books that few read, the one who makes less money than he thinks he deserves but more than he needs, the one who owns these many things, and the one who has amassed this pile of money in his investment portfolio. "*That's* who I am, who are you?"

Thus I substitute the world's meanings for God's meaning. I confuse what I say I am with what God says I am. I do not see that these are different kinds of being spoken by incomparable authors. It is a remarkable and tragic failure. It is remarkable in that I plainly cannot say what I am. For one thing, I cannot stand before myself to do the saying. For another, I am greater than any self I can say; the creation cannot be as great as its creator. It is tragic in being a morally significant struggle that disappoints the hero. The self I contrive is frail and pathetic. I shout for attention—"Look at me!"—not seeing that this makes an object of me. I claw for power, not seeing that this makes objects of others. I consume "experiences" of work, food, alcohol, sex, and sense, extravagantly, not seeing them as the escapes they are. I look into a mirror and see but a physical object—a tall, angular, aging body of doubtful attractiveness. I look into my past and see but an arbitrary and disordered list of faculties and experiences that includes sinner, saint, and everything between. The self I contrive and see is anything but an eternal, universal, and beloved child of God. I do not see the one who is literally 'per-son' (of son to God). My idea of myself is stupid and cruel, far less than what I am.

Knowing this as I do in moments of clarity, the question practically begs itself. Why do I let my anxiety get the better of me? Why do I console myself with a "castle-world" of meanings I know not to be true? Why do I welcome in my work that "world of measurement" in which I am sized and weighed, in which I am what I achieve or accumulate?[58] Why indeed do I bargain for an empty existence, for a being not mine that I know will be gravely disappointing? In a word, why do I deny my being in God? Is it because I can know the one self in experience while I must imagine the other self in faith? Is it because I want to escape the freedom for which I am responsible? Or is it because it is just easier to abandon myself to the "urgencies" of making a living and bowing to "powers"? For all of these reasons, I'm sure, and the crucial one more to which they point.

The deepest reason I deny God is that I am human. As son of the fallen Adam and Eve, I defy God in desires to be what I am not. I want to be first. I want power. I want to judge all things. I want to live forever. In short, I want to be as a god. And so I conspire with others to fashion a "world" in which something like that might happen—hence the hero system of society in which I might be "first," in which I might have "power," and in which I might be "judge." This is the mad desire of concupiscence; the sin of the first man and woman; original sin. I am this man and this woman. I forget that I am in God, that I subsist in His love. I forget that His love is the rose that grows only on the vine. To claim my being, apart from God, to think I belong to me and not to Him, is to lose this love by saying the word "mine."[59] For this, Adam and Eve and I are banished from paradise, our fates joined in suffering. As my Church reminds me, being a person, "of son" to God, I face the choice that stands before all:

> … a fundamental decision to take no account of utility and profit, career and success, as the ultimate aim of our lives, but to recognize truth and love as authentic criteria. It is a choice between living only for ourselves, and giving ourselves for something greater …[60]

Work for Being

> Work is love made visible. And if you cannot work with love but only with distaste, it is better that you should leave your work and sit at the gate of the temple and take alms from those who work with joy.[61]

Our desire for God is not rare or precious but is part of everyday life, including work. "Human work proceeds directly from persons created in the image of God and called to prolong the work of creation by subduing the earth both with and for one another."[62] Moreover, "In work, the person exercises and fulfills in part the potential inscribed in his nature. The primordial value of labor stems from man himself, its author and its beneficiary. Work is for man, not man for work."[63] Echoing this idea, Leo Tolstoy finds the want of God in everything man does:

> It only seems that people are busy with trade, with making agreements, negotiations and wars, science and the arts. There is in fact only one thing which people do; this is to search for the understanding of the moral law by which they live. And this understanding is not only the most important but the only real concern for all human kind.[64]

Gil Bailie describes our want of God as a want of "ontological density". Man, he argues, lacks being, a being he can find only in Christ: "Christ is 'the icon of the Living God,' through whose mediation we are able to imitate the One in whose image and likeness we are fashioned, which is ultimately what we long most to do."[65] It is a want that expresses itself in imitation—in what Bailie calls "mimetic desire," the desire to be Christ-like in God. This desire takes form in approaches to God; in searching, in openness to truth, in faithful practice. And this desire loses form in diversions from God; in idols of self and material possession, in narcissism, in cults of personality, in frivolous consumerism.

How can we find being, ontological density, in work? How can we forgo the meanings we make for the being God makes? What is it to *be* at work? These questions have a ready, if high-sounding, answer. We come into being at work as we are open and faithful to God.[66] The vocation we call "work" is a venue for our vocation in God. As noted, we cannot bring ourselves into being; only God can do that. And this He does by calling us to the vocations of *love, play*, and *individuation.* To *love* is to be in God's image; for He is love. In the vocation of love we unite with others in and through our differences. This is to see in the intimacies of the nuptial pair, in the camaraderie of a ball club, in the honor among thieves, and even in the fierce opposition of rivals (the beloved adversary).[67] To love is to give self to others. It is, literally, *to be* in love. To *play* is again to be in God's image; for He is the source of all creation. To play is to take part in His ongoing creation. In the vocation of play we unite in love with others to create new worlds. This is to see in the makings of games, in the imaginings of theatre, in the illuminations of conversation, and even in the regimes of war. To play is to create with others. It is, again literally, *to be* in play. Finally, to *individuate* is to become a person in God's image. In the crowning vocation of individuation, which is founded in love and elaborated in play, we take our unique place among others in society. This is to see in the various arrangements of social life, including those of family, church, tribe, club, and business. Individuation is the full measure of love and play: it is to love God by loving neighbor as self. It is *to be* in person.[68]

Strange to say, in view of my own dismal experience, work can be a way of being in God; if only we work as we might. The three vocations above lead to God; they answer the commandment of Christ to love God with all one's mind, heart, and soul and to love one's neighbor as self. I offer a hypothetical case in point. I invite four friends to help me build a stone patio at the back of my house. It is involved and taxing work. There is a design to draw up, a budget to manage, stones to purchase and transport, an excavation to dig, a drain field of crushed stone to lay, a top layer of sand to lay and to roll, guide lines to set and chalk, edges to lay, stones to cut and lay in a pattern, and sand to fill the cracks. What would it take for my friends and me to find ourselves in this work?

In the first place it would take answering the call of love—to work "all for one," as a division in unity, and to work as "one for all," as a unity in division. It would be to reach across our differences (of ability, skill, and inclination) in community. And in this community it would be to hold fast to our unique being as persons. To let this happen is to let God into our lives, for He is the ground for the unity in division and division in unity that is love. We see God's love in our lives as we together create our world. Our "world" is the one we make in word and deed—the world of birds and boats, fishes and phones, reptiles and refrigerators, mammals and marionettes, and in this case, patios. The love of world-making that reaches across personal differences of experience, ability, and will is possible because God made us in His image as sentient and creative beings joined in one body of humanity. He made us to love, free to overcome our differences by giving ourselves to one another. His love is the source from which our loves draw; our loves are but a faint and imperfect copy of His. My friends and I, in our patio adventure, have His supreme love to draw on as we reach across our differences to join efforts. His love and ours are both a condition and fulfillment of our work.

However, while love is necessary, it is not enough. For my friends and me to find ourselves in building the patio we must be one with the work. We must enter it pure of heart, without preemption or expectation, and free of diverting concerns (e.g., costs, debts incurred or repaid, increased property value, admiration and envy of neighbors, risks of fatigue or injury).[69] For as long as it lasts the work must be our reality, our life, our creation—in a word, our being. The patio must be for us *sui generis;* not just *a* patio like any other, but *the* patio of our being. This is an idea of the work as play. And to play is, again, to welcome God into our lives. Safe in His love we leave behind the worries of ordinary existence (of sustenance, physical safety, etc.) and accept the "worries" of patio-building (which aren't worries at all). Moreover, it is not we who create (we do not have the power to make something from nothing), but He that creates through us. Although we may not recognize it as such, the joy that my friends and I experience in our labors together—a joy of creative play that is a mystery to social science[70]—is the joy of being in God. My friends and I have this joy to draw on as we muscle our way through the day. This joy, like the love it presupposes, is both a condition and fulfillment of our work.

And finally, while love and play are necessary and go a long way, they are not enough. For my friends and me to find ourselves in building the patio we must each become our own person. This we must do each in our own way, by establishing our own relations with others in the group, by taking our place in the life of the whole. In practice we must work out the details of getting the work done; for example, one to design, one or two to measure and stake the dimensions, a few to transport materials, a few to excavate, lay down rock and sand, and role the surface flat, and finally all together to move, cut, lay, and grout the stones. Our division of labor is significant, not for its details (which could vary widely), but for its individuation. Our division of labor is the culmination of love and play; the result of reaching across differences to form a creative unity. At its end lies our group and person in full—our group an integral coordination of creative effort, our person a unique and valued locus of creative effort. For my friends and me to achieve such an individuation in our patio adventure is again to welcome God into our lives. For like the love and play of which it is the culmination, individuation is also an image of God. In God we are truly and completely a person of inalienable dignity and inestimable worth. And in God we are truly and completely joined in one human body—one humanity. Thus in God we come to fruition as His unique and beloved child joined with His other children in the unity of His creation. While this ultimate and true vocation remains beyond our earthly grasp, it is what my friends and I reach for when we come together to build the patio. We reach for this heaven in our work on earth. As noted above, according to Tolstoy this is the (largely) unconscious aim of everything we do. And to the extent we succeed, we come to something that is no longer "work", but is something more like play, something divine. As Mark Twain notes:

> Who was it who said, "Blessed is the man who has found his work"? Whoever it was he had the right idea in his mind. Mark you, he says his work—not somebody else's work. The work that is really a man's own work is play and not work at all.[71]

While the example of my friends and me building a patio reveals possibilities of being in God, and thereby gives answer to the question "Who am I?", it hardly captures the everyday realities of work such as described earlier about the writing of this chapter. Even in work among friends, with ready prospects of love, play, and individuation, we fail to be what we can be. More difficult are the circumstances of work in daily life when more is at stake. Think of the preemptions, intrusions, and concerns of ego that divert us from God: that *demean love* by replacing our true unity of being in God, in which each person is an infinitely valued and inalienable element of His creation, with the ersatz unity of business organizations, in which each individual is a contingent and expendable member of a workforce; that *diminish play* by confounding the inner life of creation with outer instrumentalities of purpose, supervision, and evaluation; and that severely *limit individuation* by defining people not as persons (i.e., "of son" to God) but as human resources (i.e., economic factors of production to deploy as circumstances of production dictate and worth only what the market will pay for their services). Were we better than we are—were we faithful and able to love, play, and individuate as God intends—we might be more than we are. However, because we are far from perfect, because we are corrupted by sin, our being in God is evanescent. It appears only as we love our neighbor as self in God.

In God, I Trust

A chapter on being must end in the first person. Although we work together we come to be in our own person. I began with the problem "Who am I?" I end by noting that as every problem is to understand in its proper context, this problem is to understand in the context of the living God. The "who" that I am is revealed by the incarnation, by the human form taken by God in Christ. Christ's revelation of the Trinitarian God (as Father, Son, and Holy Spirit) is the foundation for my self-understanding. The Trinitarian God, Who is division in unity (three persons in one God) and unity in division (one God in three persons), is the source and perfection of love, play, and individuation. It is to God that my earthly strivings reach.

To the question "Who am I?" comes the sure and final answer that "I am a child of God." In this answer, which quiets my longing, my problem of being is not existential but providential. It is to discern what the Father calls from me. It is to figure out how I fit into His kingdom, both here on earth and in life ever after. In this matter my answer can only be my own. And, in this matter my work can only be my own. But with this idiosyncrasy granted, what I must do is what every person must do. First I must *relax*. I must give up my mad scramble for worldly meaning and be still in God. I must listen for His answer—let His love hold me in union with others; let His love free me to create with others; and let His love define my place in relation to others. Second I must *obey*. I must do as Christ commands: Love the Lord God with all my heart, mind and soul; and love my neighbor as myself. To do these two things—to relax and to obey—is to come into being, is to realize the three aspects of my being: I *love* by reaching across differences to find unity with others; I *play* by joining others to create new worlds; and I *individuate* by finding my place in society with others.

Of course Christ's simple command could not be more difficult to obey. To love God with all my heart, mind, and soul and to love my neighbor as myself is to put God at the center of my life and to regard my self as equal and one with others. It is to do what I repeatedly show myself unable to do. It is to abandon my self to God. It is to admit that I am not god but that He is God. It is to abandon the measures and grades by which I esteem and console myself. It is to see that the prizes of the world are for naught and that the more fervently I have sought them the more completely I denied my being in God. It is to see that I am human, fallen and my own worst enemy. And finally, it is to see that I do not have a choice about God, not a practical one anyway. Either I accept His offer of being, or I die.

In the end I see that my being at work is a drama of whether or not I can fulfill my vocation to give myself to God who has set paradise before me. Will I again stray from Him in my chase of meaning? Will I again sacrifice my being in Him to worldly idols of fortune, fame, adulation, and power, among others? Or can I, in the wisdom of faith, avoid the obstacles that work puts before my being in God—among these its purposes and instrumentalities, its objectifications of persons and relations, its ruthless efficiency, its relentless profiteering, and its siren call to consumerism? How difficult it is to keep God in mind, to dwell not in a fallen world of selfishness but in a risen world of love, play, and individuation. This is not to deny concerns for efficiency, effectiveness, quality, and profit at work, but it is to see them not as ends in themselves, but as means to the highest end of being in God. While it may seem the better part of realism to think that work is bigger than we are and that we must adapt ourselves to it, the truth is to see, again with Pope John Paul II, that we are not for work but that work is for us.

Chapter 3

Why the Center Holds

Mary Parker Follett was perhaps our wisest student of the corporation and of its management. She described the manager's job as leadership, not in the conventional and over-simple terms of command and control (of bossing people around) or charisma and inspiration (of wowing people into commitment), but in the exacting terms of the "total situation" of the corporation in which the contributions of each and every person are articulated and valued to form an "integrative unity." She put in for a tall order:

> The leader must be the leader of a coherent group, of men who are finding their material welfare, their most effective expression, their spiritual satisfaction, through their relations to one another, through the functioning of the group to which they belong.[72]

It is a worthwhile goal, arguably *the* worthwhile goal, but how can managers bring it about? In her studies of business and government Follett came upon managers who occasionally came close, but neither they nor she could say how. Wrote Follett: "There are two fundamental problems for business management: first, to define the essential nature of the total situation; secondly, how to pass from one total situation to another. I think we have answered the first fairly satisfactorily ... We have not yet answered the second ..."[73]

Managers who are honest with themselves must look upon their leadership in grateful wonder. Their experience is a mariner's nightmare. Tossed about on stormy seas, with the barest of charts and few guiding landmarks, they captain a ship that is complex and does not keep its shape and they captain a crew that is varied and not altogether un-motley. And yet, somehow, despite their miscalculations of navigation, they awake to find the crew doing yeoman's work (often on their own initiative, with little direction, and with not enough thanks) and the ship aright and mostly on course. Their mostly successful leadership must seem more happenstance than plan.

This chapter is about the wonder of the corporation, that idealized by Follett and that realized by managers in spite of themselves. How does a corporation meet conditions that no one quite understands? How does a corporation survive the miscalculations of its leaders? And why are workers stubbornly faithful to their all-too-human managers? In sum: What keeps a corporation together? This chapter is about what explains the integrity and perseverance of the corporation amidst its storm-tossed passage. And this chapter is about what guidance is needed from leadership and from the law to hold the corporation to its course.

Dark Matter Mystery

The questions about the corporation above are mysteries, even to students of law and business. In law, the corporation is an abstraction—"an idealized essence that has no existence outside the virtual legal space in which it is produced...the basic definition of a corporation is an investment vehicle for the pooling of money and labor whose purpose is singular—to maximize profits."[74] As David Millon describes, the twisting history of legal thought about the corporation has culminated in an idea of the corporation as a natural aggregate of individuals, a so-called "nexus of contracts."[75] In economics, the corporation is no less an abstraction—a structure of persons joined under authority. As R.H. Coase describes, "A firm consists of the system of relationships which comes into existence when the direction of resources is dependent on an entrepreneur."[76] In both law and economics, the corporation is held together by contracts that align inducements to contributions on behalf of the whole.[77] The job of the manager therefore is to get the inducements-contributions balance right, or at least right enough. However, while this image of the corporation is matter-of-fact (for it is certainly true that the corporation is a nexus of contracts), it leaves the corporation itself unexplained. As noted long ago by the sociologist Emile Durkheim and again recently by the economist Kenneth Arrow, such reductive concepts of the corporation cannot explain how the elements of the corporation become organized—how they comprise a division of labor, needs, and goods.[78] Economic organization cannot be its own explanation. Moreover, such reductive concepts cannot explain the intrinsic value of the corporation—for the satisfaction and even joy that is part of every collective endeavor. There is no word about such things as filial love, affinity, communion, or altruism. The corporation is thus construed without human dimension, as a financial abstraction, as a "nexus of contracts." While such a construal might appeal to those who would manage a corporation without human concern, as though it was only a financial portfolio, it could hardly be imagined by those who know that a corporation depends upon the trust and goodwill of its members, that it would collapse as a house of cards should its members work to contract only.[79]

Indeed, the mystery of the corporation deepens the more we look into it. It is not only the artificial and rational instrument described by students of law and business. It is at the same time its own being, a vital unity having its own laws and needs. This essential unity was the distinctive concern of Mary Follett who looked into organizations more deeply than most to see their inner *functional relating*:

> Functional relating is the continuing process of self-creating coherence. Most of my philosophy is contained in that sentence. You can take that sentence, I believe, as a test for any part of business organization or business management. If you have the right kind of functional relating, you will have a process which will create a unity which will lead to further unities—a self-creating progression.[80]

Thus the corporation is more than a nexus of contracts. To the contrary, it is a complex dynamic that somehow integrates the rational imperatives of economic organization with the vital imperatives of its own organism.[81] The corporation is something to which managers must come with a dual sensibility—with intellect to grasp its rational organization and with intuition to grasp its organism. And upon these graspings they must work alchemy—to secure organization by imposing structures and purposes and to nurture organism by giving it resources and room to grow. How this is done no one can quite say, not students of law or business, nor yet practitioners.

The mystery of the corporation can be compared to that of the cosmos in astronomy. Of the cosmos there is much to see. Moons gather around planets, planets around stars, stars around galaxies, and galaxies around each other, in a texture that has been extensively mapped. The puzzle for astronomers is that these visible elements do not have the mass and therefore gravity necessary to account for their texture. This unaccounted coherence has led astronomers to postulate an invisible "dark matter" to supplement visible matter to explain the cosmos. It is a humbling idea, not least because this undiscovered dark matter is estimated to comprise upwards of 90% of the total. The unaccounted coherence of the corporation challenges in the same way. Its visible elements—in particular, its collection of individual interests and its nexus of contracts—cannot account for its integrity and uncanny adaptability, for its devotion to cause, and for its resilient tolerance of mismanagement. Something else must be at work to hold the corporation together, some analogous dark matter invisible to the eye.

Of the Body

Language husbands its wisdom. According to the *Oxford English Dictionary*, the word 'corporation' is a noun of action deriving from the word incorporation [ad. late L. *incorporationem*] which it defines as: **1.a.** the action of incorporating two or more things, or one thing *with* (*in*, *into*) another; the process or condition of being so incorporated; union in or into one body. And **2. a.** the action or process of forming into a community or corporation; *esp.* the formation of a legal corporation or body politic.[82] Could this definition of the corporation as "union in or into one body" be the key to the mystery of its integrity and vitality? Could it be that the corporation is literally rooted in the body, in our flesh and blood lives? Corporation and corporeal are one word; are they one idea? More particularly, and intriguingly, could it be that what is essentially "incorporated" is the one God-given division of the body; namely, that of male and female? Perhaps the matter that holds the corporation together is not "dark" at all, but is instead the "light" of love that begins where all human love begins, in bodily union of male and female.

Before the reader rejects this idea as too remote, or as too corny, or even as too racy, let us hasten back to Follett's observation above that: "If you have the right kind of functional relating, you will have a process which will create a unity which will lead to further unities—a self-creating progression." While Follett does not say what the right kind of functional relating is, much less that it is of male and female, she supposes that for every organization there is a unity of unities and that every organization grows and develops as a "self-creating progression" from lower- to higher-level unities. Such a supposition is crucial because it insists upon the sort of possibility entertained here; that elementary functional relations are paramount and from them arise and develop the higher-level functional relations. With the idea of incorporation, could the elementary functional relation, the unity of unities, be that of male and female?

Although concerned mainly with the science of organization, Follett appreciated the spiritual dimension of organization as well. She wrote of the need for "spiritual satisfaction,"[83] of the need for leadership that appealed to the "recesses of the spirit" and connected one to "the hidden springs of all life,"[84] and of the need to temper selfish interests by thinking of ourselves as "members of the highest unity with which we are capable of identifying ourselves"[85] Such spiritual resonances suggest a bridge between science and faith. What if we brought Follett's science of organization back to the origins of human organization in Genesis, back to the shadowy beginnings of creation known to faith? What might faith and reason together tell us about the dark matter mystery of the corporation?

"In the beginning," according to the Book of Genesis, "... God created man in his *own* image, in the image of God he created him; male and female he created him."[86] By defining Adam and Eve as male and female "in one flesh," Genesis furnishes a precise definition of 'sex' in both its noun form, as a division of male and female, and its verb form, as a uniting of these in the image of God. Human society is established as a single living organism, as a whole made of the functional relating of male and female parts. Moreover, according to Genesis, by incarnating God in "one flesh," we are distinguished from every other "thing that creepeth on the earth." Where other animals join in couplings that typically last only as long as the acts themselves, we join in a divine union that is renewed in coupling and that lasts a lifetime in spirit if not in fact.[87]

This claim of incorporation—that human society embodies God by its functional relating of male and female—is thus a historical one that reaches back to the first seeds of society in creation. If Follett is correct that social unity is a "self-creating progression," then we should find the functional unity of male and female in all human societies, past and present. In this unity we should find the "dark matter" that holds the corporation together. Upon this point, as upon so many others, faith and science agree. For her part the Church tells the truth that the nuptial pair is

> ... *the original cell of social life*. It is the natural society in which husband and wife are called to give themselves in love and in the gift of life. Authority, stability, and a life of relationships within the family constitute the foundations for freedom, security, and fraternity within society.[88]

And for her part, science tells the (always provisional) story of how this truth has come to be. According to current thinking, it is a story both of evolutionary continuity, in which we conserve patterns of mammalian and especially primate society, and of evolutionary discontinuity, in which we take leave of these patterns to establish a pattern all our own. In total, it is the story of our human creation in the image of God, a story of a flowering of three distinct levels of functional relating of male and female.[89]

Love's Flower

The first or "primary" level of functional relating and unity is given by three universal elements of sexual being—female care of young, female mate choice, and male competition—that have been conserved through tens of millions of years of mammalian evolution and that comprise the primary organizing dynamic of mammalian social life.[90] Together these elements comprise a functional dynamic of opposition and affirmation. These elements at once divide the sexes as to task and orientation *and* unite the sexes in the vital imperative to reproduce. This mutuality of male and female is the ground of sociality throughout the animal kingdom. In this we do as other animals do.

A second and higher level of functional relating and unity arose uniquely in our kind when we took leave from our mammalian ancestors by enlarging and extending the primary relation of male and female. This happened during the Pleistocene Era as a result of our move from the rich and relatively safe biome of forest trees to the hardscrabble and more dangerous biome of the open savannah, a move that brought further differentiation and specialization of the sexes and that occasioned two distinctively human adaptations of society. One was *same-sex grouping*: a tendency for men to group with men and for women to group with women. Although characteristic of men and women alike, same-sex grouping figured differently in the lives of each. For men, the group enabled hunting on the open savannah by coordinating efforts to stalk, mob, and overcome the big game needed to feed and clothe the community. For women, the group facilitated sharing of food and other resources (including defense) in care of children. The second and related adaptation to Pleistocene life on the savannah was *family*: that all-important reproducing unit of the species that consists of a woman with children attached more or less exclusively to a man.[91] Family adapted the species to conditions where men in groups left the village to hunt and to explore and women stayed closer to home to gather nearby foods and to care for children. Family promised woman a man to return with food, to defend her and her children from attack, and to help with child-care. And family promised man a woman with whom he could mate and from whom he could receive comfort.[92] Thus, in this secondary sexual order of same-sex groups and family, there is again a functional dynamic of opposition and affirmation in which each creates and meets the need of the other.[93]

Finally, the most surprising and surpassing level of functional relating and unity is that of mind and culture. At this level particularly we fulfill our being in the image of God. As we've seen, the primary and secondary sexual orders of human society are universals rooted in the body—the primary order a mammalian trait built into a body plan of reproductively central females and reproductively aspiring males; the secondary order a human trait tied to a suite of hominid adaptations to savannah life. The tertiary sexual order of human society consists of features that vary from group to group. These are not physical elements rooted in genes, but mental elements rooted in ideas about how people should live in the group.

Culture is conception, an act of mind. It is a communal exercise of the human capacity to make and use symbols. This capacity may have arisen early in group life as hominid ancestors turned natural communicative signs (e.g., grunts, footfalls, cries) into conceptual symbols (e.g., words, gestures, dances). As suggested by Susanne Langer, the first symbols of culture were probably visual and auditory images of the group (e.g., choric shouts, communal dances) invented to maintain the integrity of the group amid the isolations of an open and challenging savannah life.[94] With an image of the group in mind, people could remain in the group mentally despite being separated from it physically. With an image of the group in mind, people could wander farther from the group and operate more autonomously on its behalf. And with an image of the group in mind, people could coordinate their efforts at a distance, each person knowing his/her place and part in the whole. A hunting group, for example, could exploit a wider range and capture larger animals. Thus, a tertiary or cultural social order exists whenever people act toward one another *as members of a group*---that is, when they act in awareness of their own and others' roles in the group.[95]

Despite its seemingly endless variations across time and place, the tertiary order of mind and culture retains its roots in the incorporation of male and female. This is in two crucial respects. *First*, the tertiary order is dedicated to the primary and secondary orders upon which it is built. Cultures sanction ideas about social life, especially about relations between the sexes, to enable people to live peaceably in the best interest of the group. Thus, for examples, values of chivalry support respectful competition among men and respectful treatment of women; marriage vows sanctify women's mate choice and reinforce monogamy and family; and community laws about rape, sexual harassment, sexual perversion, incest, child abuse, child custody and child support protect men and women from each other. *Second*, the tertiary order is itself an incorporation of male and female. Mind and culture are animated and organized as a functional relating of male and female elements. The human mind is, in everything that it knows, a play of reason and intuition. As psychoanalyst Karl Stern has observed, this duality of mind results from a sexual companionability that begins in the body and extends to our whole encounter with the world:

> The polarity of the sexes is based on body-build and organ function but not confined to it. The male principle enables us to master our relationship with reality, to solve our problems rationally. Woman acts and reacts out of the dark mysterious depths of the unconscious; i.e. affectively, intuitively. This is no judgment of value but a statement of fact.[96]

By the same token, culture is, in its myriad incarnations, a play of hierarchy (born of male concern for position and status) and natural community (born of female concern for life and nurture). As anthropologist Margaret Mead observed, the sexual organization of culture is universal, even while it varies in details (here a strong family structure, there a weak one, here powerful male groups, there weak ones, here strong monogamy, there mild polygamy, etc…).[97] This sexual dynamism of culture recalls that of the corporation noted at the outset of the article between *organization* and *organism*. We saw that the manager brings to this dynamism a two-fold sensitivity which grasps organization by reason and organism by intuition. In this we now see a meeting of mind and culture in the functional relating of male and female.

Thus the creation of man as male and female in God's image let loose a flowering of functional relating that has culminated in the societies we know today, including that of the corporation. To be human is not only to stand apart from other beings in divine splendor; it is also to stand with other beings in an evolutionary continuity. *Culture* and *mind* are definitive human images of God's creative will, and *same-sex groups* and *family* are distinctive human forms of society, but these could not exist apart from mammalian sexual order—of *female care of young*, *female mate choice*, and *male competition*. Human history consists of the progressive functional relating of male and female. Design a human life without the primary elements of sexual order—without women choosing mates wisely and caring for children, or without men competing fairly for women's attention and favor—and you design a life without same-sex groups and family, a life without mind and culture, a life hardly human. Remote though this deep human history may seem, we bring it to mind unconsciously when we speak of a corporation, as we often do, as a "family". This is no metaphor, but a truth wiser than we know. The alchemy of organization and organism of today's well-functioning corporation elaborates and extends that of the first family of creation. It is a conservation of our life and good.

To Garden Eden

Although founded upon a great insight about functional unity, Mary Follett's ideas about the corporation were limited by their silence on two questions: What is the primary unity of human being? (With what does functional relating begin?) And, what is the final unity of human being? (To what does functional relating lead?) Ever the worldly philosopher, Follett may have thought such questions too big or too existential to occupy a manager. But lacking answers to these questions, she was puzzled by conflicting interests of unity across units and levels of the corporation. How could demands for integration within a work group or department be squared with demands for integration across work groups or departments? Or, how could demands for integration within a corporation be tallied with demands for integration across corporations? Unless founded upon a common primary unity and unless oriented to a single final unity, the demands for unity across units and levels are likely to conflict. Integration in one place is likely to come at the expense of integration in another. Concerned by such unproductive conflicts, Follett urged contesting parties to qualify their selfish interests by thinking of themselves as "members of the highest unity possible" so that they together might achieve the greatest integration possible.

Follett's puzzlement is answered by faith. The highest unity possible, in a corporation or anywhere else, exists when primary and final unity are the same; namely, when we are formed in the image of God in union of male and female. History began with the perfect unity of Genesis, of Adam and Eve in one flesh. History since has been a struggle to reclaim paradisiacal perfection.[98] It has been a struggle because, since the fall of Adam and Eve in Eden's Garden—since their rejection of God in favor of themselves—we are ever losing sight of God and thereby of our highest unity. But history is to learn so that it will not be repeated. In everything we do there is opportunity for redemption. This is true even and perhaps especially of the corporation. In and through its activity we are called to incorporation, to the divine mystery of love in male and female.

The call to incorporation begins in the union of male and female. As we have seen, social life is a consummation of male and female—at the lowest level of bodies, in sexual intercourse; at a higher level of persons, in the play of sex roles; at a still higher-level of groups, in the play of same-sex groups and family;

and at the highest level of mind and culture, in the play of reason and intuition and in the play of organization and organism. Thus the flower of love between male and female is to recognize and cherish. At the primary level of male and female reproductive roles, this is to guard female mate choice (e.g., by corporate policies against sexual harassment, by enforcement of civil laws against rape), to sanction free and fair competition of males for females (e.g., by encouraging and recognizing merit in organizations), and to support female care of young (e.g., by family-friendly policies such as maternity leave, flexible and part-time employment; by a 'family wage' that allows husbands to support wives who choose to stay home with children). At the secondary level of same-sex groups and family, this is to recognize men's and women's instinct to join their kind in mutual support and to meet their opposite member in a family (e.g., by allowing the sexes to coalesce and segregate in the workplace, by supporting family life among employees). And at the tertiary level of mind and culture, this is to encourage both male and female values and sensibilities (e.g., in mind by tempering male analysis and reason with female judgment and intuition, and in culture by leavening male structure and system with female compassion and spontaneity).[99] In sum, the good of the corporation is the good of the union of male and female in God. The good is to let men and women be true to their bodies, to let them find sanctuary in male and female groups, and to let them complete one another in the family. To let men be men and women be women is to let them be gifts to one another.

Looking more generally we see that the call to incorporation answers Christ's two-fold commandment of love: "You shall love the Lord your God with all your heart, and with all your soul, and with all your mind. This is the great and first commandment. And a second is like it, You shall love your neighbor as yourself."[100] God's children all, we are not together in order unless and until we love one another in obedient love of God our Father. This is the foundation of the most basic term of organization, *hierarchy*, which means 'sacred order.' Its godless alternative is *anarchy*. Christ's commandment is no abstract or empty directive, but a concrete principle to govern every relationship in the corporation—including those of superior and subordinate, line and staff, buyer and seller, investor and board of directors, business and government, and even competitor and competitor. Every human relation is concerned not only with the business at hand but also with the business of eternal salvation.[101] Indeed this last concern makes possible the first because it conjures a trustworthy order of mutual concern, based on truth and justice, in which disparate interests can be integrated. Knowing that their commerce is to judge by the eyes of God, and knowing that others love them as they love themselves, business partners can trust that they will not be taken advantage of or compromised: subordinates can trust superiors to act with compassion, buyers can trust sellers to represent their products fairly, investors can trust managers' intentions, and industry rivals can trust one another to compete fairly according to the rules. Thus God is the supreme unity—the unity of unities—within which every interest at every level can be integrated. This is "highest level" unity to which Follett alluded in hopes of full and complete coordination and control in business.

These ideas matter because how we think about the corporation determines the laws make about it and the mores we bring to its management.[102] In a word, these ideas comprise a moral foundation for the corporation. In relation to God's plan for us, the corporation can be either a consecration or a desecration. It is a consecration when, as described above, it affirms and fulfills God's image of male and female in one flesh. It is a desecration when it denies or depletes this image. Sadly, too much thinking about the corporation today desecrates this image by regarding people abstractly and instrumentally as "litigants" or as "human resources" rather than concretely and essentially as male and female persons. By isolating them from one another in abstraction this thinking today denies their complementary union in body and soul. The worry in such thinking is not simply that it is cold and calculating, but that it is inhumane. Where God created human love and life in the one flesh of male and female, such thinking destroys this love and life. By not incorporating male and female in God, such thinking robs the corporation of the functional relating and essential dynamism of human life.[103]

Today this desecration is allied with a "political correctness" which denies sexual being altogether. Here the idea is that being male or female is a "social construction," a subjective incidental of "gender," not a truth of being in God.[104] In strict formulations this view forbids all but the most undeniable differences between the sexes, on the grounds that these might be used to justify "inequalities" in organizational roles and/or outcomes (which to this view can never be justified). Thus sexual equality does not mean what it would mean in a total view of human life; namely, that men and women should take equally important parts in society. It means instead that men and women should lead the same lives with the same outcomes and that this should be true in every corner and at every level of society. To this way of thinking, there can be no general functional relation between men and women because there are no general differences between them to relate and put to work. That humankind is divided into male and female parts is supposed not to be important, except perhaps to heterosexuals who enjoy the pleasure and occasional offspring that come of their meeting. In less strict formulations this view, differences between men and women are acknowledged in complaint. Most often this takes the form of a bias for men's lives, in the belief that men get the better of life, both at work and at home. This desecration of our being in God is harder to dismiss because it contains a grain of truth. If one judges all human life in the terms by which men are judged (both by themselves and by women)—namely, in terms of accomplishment, wealth, or status—then men will be favored and will be judged superior to women. It could hardly be otherwise because, as noted earlier, women do not care about the same things and do not play the same games as men. But such a reckoning ignores the half of life to judge in the terms by which women are compared (both by themselves and by men)—namely, in terms of nurture in care and concern for others. This is to forget that human being depends upon the reciprocity of male and female and, therefore, that one half cannot be more important or more worthwhile than the other. This is also to miss the irony that what is male begins in the female. The male embryo begins life as a female until a flood of testosterone masculinizes it. Moreover, it is the bodily creativeness of a mother that grants a male child his own mysterious law of becoming. His eventual traits of assertion, analysis, reason, and organization are founded upon her receptivity, feeling, intuition, and organism. And, finally, this is to forget that as complements, male and female anticipate and conjure one another. There is femaleness in every male and maleness in every female by which each can appreciate the other.

Lost on many legal and business scholars today is a truth about our being an image of God in the union of male and female; namely, that there is and can be no sexual equality of sameness. We cannot expect to find sexual sameness in the corporation any more than we can expect to find it in the home, or in the nursery, or in any other corner of life. We are joined in society everywhere by the functional relating of male and female, a functional relating made possible and productive by their differences. We cannot choose this for it is built into our being. This is not to deny that men and women can and should be allowed every opportunity to take part and succeed in whatever life they wish for themselves—i.e., that their dignity and rights as individual persons must be primary. But it is to recognize that as society everywhere arises and seeks its end in the incorporation of male and female in God, men and women are bound to seek and enjoy different lives.[105] Such is the difference of life – *viva la difference.*

Finally, we can note that by identifying the nuptial foundations of the corporation we add our affidavit to those of the Church in support of a theology of the corporation. With the deepening of her social doctrine, especially in the last century with Pope Pius XI's encyclical *Rerum Novarum* and Pope John Paul II's encyclicals *Laborem Exercens* and *Centesimus Annus*,[106] the Church has emphasized the crucial role of the corporation in salvation history. Following in this vein, theologians today describe the corporation as a "community of work" patterned after the community of the Holy Trinity;[107] as a "double finality" oriented both to natural and supernatural ends;[108] and as a "mediating institution" of moral solidarity and common good in keeping with God's will for man.[109] These ideas share in the conviction that the corporation must be ordered to God; and in particular that its familiar concerns for profit and shareholder-wealth must not be taken as its ends in themselves, but must instead be taken as its means to the end of fulfilling man's being in God.[110] This chapter is one more effort to bring the corporation—an institution of immense power in our lives—into the light of the faith that illuminates and informs all things. To see the foundations of the modern corporation in the nuptial pair is to see the corporation more fully as an instrument of God's plan for us.

Conclusion

To the question of what keeps the corporation together, and to the question of what law and business must take care to protect and nurture, comes a simple answer: love. Human unity is incorporation, is God imaged by the union of male and female. This union may be the one flesh of the nuptial pair, or it may be the body of the Church, or it may be the body of a corporation or any other social institution. But always it is a body of male and female elements; a unity developed upon their functional relating. Our human being in God is the ground of what Follett called the "continuing process of self-creating coherence." But we can and must be more precise than Follett, to recognize that the coherence of the corporation is not literally "self-created" but is a realization of the love built into our being male and female. Thus faith informs and enlarges scientific reason. Where Follett delineates the key concept of functional relating, faith teaches what functional relating is and where it comes from. According to faith, the corporation images God in its union of male and female.

Love enjoins us to God; "Thy will be done." Our relation to God began with His creation of us in His image and thus with His investing in us some of his creative power. Our responsibility in everything we do is to enlarge and extend His love through this gift of grace. As described in Genesis, our creative power begins in the union of male and female in which we are an image God. As we have seen again and again, ours is a two-fold power that involves at once the creative agency of the female to nurture and let things grow by their own laws and the creative agency of the male to make things by reason and will. This is the two-fold power upon which legal scholars and corporate leaders must rely if they are take the full measure of the functional relating and unity of the corporation. And with this clarification of what scholars and leaders must appreciate, we are returned to Mary Follett who saw for the leader the greatest aim of all, an aim that recalls Christ's commandment of love to us all:

> ... businessmen can ... put into practice certain fundamental principles. They may be making useful products; in addition to that they may be helping the individuals in their employ to further development; but even beyond all these things, by helping in solving the problems of organization, they are helping to solve the problems of human relations, and that is certainly the greatest task man has been given on this planet.[111]

Chapter 4

Thy Will Be Done?

> Into the public consciousness creeps the suspicion that our whole attitude to power is wrong; more, that our growing power is a growing threat to ourselves...In the coming epoch, the essential problem will no longer be that of increasing power—though power will continue to increase at an ever swifter tempo—but of curbing it. The core of the new epoch's intellectual task will be to integrate power into life in such a way that man can employ power without forfeiting his humanity. For he will have only two choices; to match the greatness of his power with the strength of his humanity, or to surrender his humanity to power and perish.[112]

> ... what you receive from your leader does not come from him, but from the "recesses of the spirit." Whoever connects me with the hidden springs of all life, whoever increases the sense of life in me, he is my leader.[113]

Two Puzzles of Power

Power—the ability to get things done—is said by many to be the key to success in business and indeed everywhere else in life. According to U.S. President Richard Nixon, no stranger to power or to success:

> It is not enough for a leader to know the right thing. He must be able to do the right thing. The...leader without the judgment or perception to make the right decisions fails for lack of vision. The one who knows the right thing but cannot achieve it fails because he is ineffectual. The great leader needs...the capacity to achieve.[114]

And so power, the ability of business leaders to get things done, would seem to be an unalloyed good; something always to seek and exercise; something always to want more of, like life itself. But this is not how power is seen by many or most people. To the contrary, says Rosabeth Kanter, "Power is America's last dirty word. It is easier to talk about money—and much easier to talk about sex—than it is to talk about power."[115] And according to John Gardiner "In this country—and in most other democracies—power has such a bad name that many good people persuade themselves they want nothing to do with it."[116] This is the first puzzle of power: its ambivalence. Why are we reluctant about the plain good of getting things done?

A second puzzle of power relates to and indeed may underlie the first. This is that most people judge power not by its achievements but by its ethics. For them it is crucial that leaders reach for goals in the right way. "Tyrants," who are cruel and pitiless in their exercise of power, are condemned. This is to see, for example, in *Fortune Magazine*, which "celebrates" such leaders with its occasional rankings of the "Toughest Bosses." It distinguishes these leaders by their "penchant for psychological oppression," and by their "sadistic way of making a point, say, or a bullying quality that can transform underlings into quivering masses of Jell-O" (10/18/1993). Atop its 1993 ranking was Steve Jobs, founder and CEO of Apple Computer, who it described as a "brilliant man" whose "drive for perfection is so strong that employees who don't meet his expectations face blistering verbal attacks that can eventually burnout even the most motivated." Ranked second was Linda Wachner, head of Warnaco, so-called "queen of impatience" who, according to one story, "lashed out at a meeting of executives from the women's clothing group. Angered by their performance, she declared: "You're eunuchs. How can your wives stand you? You've got nothing between your legs." The disdain expressed for these leaders contrasts with the esteem held for rather different leaders. Writing in the *Harvard Business Review*, Jim Collins identified two qualities of power that distinguish the very best leaders—personal humility and intense professional will. Pointing to Darwin Smith, CEO of Kimberly-Clarke, and Colman Mockler, CEO of Gillette Collins found, on the one hand, humble men who are modest and shun praise, who channel ambition into the company and not self, and who take personal responsibility for poor results; and on the other hand, fiercely resolved men who will do whatever it takes to produce superb long-term results, who set the standard of building an enduring great company, and who credit others for success. Comparing the two images of power, the toughest bosses and the humble and resolved leaders, we are left to puzzle about what else there is to power besides "getting things done"? What is behind our ethical intuitions about power? Is there a wisdom that we bring to power, a wisdom written on the heart? And if so, what is it and who did the writing?

Power, Authority, and Responsibility

We are puzzled by the moral dimension of power for the same reason that we are puzzled by most things; because we think about it in the wrong way.

According to social scientists, power is a natural and thus morally neutral phenomenon. French and Raven defined social power as "the resultant of two forces set up by the act of [social agent] O: one in the direction of O's influence attempt and another resisting force in the opposite direction."[117] Warren Bennis and Burt Nanus define power as the "energy needed to initiate and sustain action, or, to put it another way, the capacity to translate intention into reality and sustain it."[118] And Jeffrey Pfeffer confirms this natural image by defining power as "the potential ability to influence behavior, to change the course of events, to overcome resistance, and to get people to do things they would not otherwise do."[119] By identifying power with nature—with how the world is—instead of with justice—with how the world ought to be—these ideas strip power of its moral dimensions, of its connections to what is right and good. Such amoral reasoning about power turns to amoral practice in ideas about how to manage power in organizations. Robert Cialdini, for example, trumpets a "science of persuasion" whose research shows that persuasion "is governed by basic principles that can be taught, learned, and applied. By mastering these principles, executives can bring scientific rigor to the business of securing consensus, cutting deals, and winning concessions."[120] And answering his own question of what it means to manage with power, Jeffrey Pfeffer says it means: 1) to diagnose the political landscape; 2) to figure out what other powerful actors want; 3) to understand that to get things done you need more power than those who oppose you, and 4) to understand the strategies and tactics of developing and using power.[121] Without coming right out and saying so, these ideas turn power into an instrument or tool to judge only or mainly by the ends to which it is put.[122] As Alasdair MacIntyre has observed:

> Managers... and most writers about management conceive of themselves as morally neutral characters whose skills enable them to devise the most efficient means of achieving whatever end is proposed. Whether a given manager is effective or not is on the dominant view a quite different question from that of the morality of the ends which his effectiveness serves or fails to serve.[123]

To resolve the puzzles of power we must understand its moral dimension. As has been said, power consists in the ability to *take action* in the world—to get things done. But what has not yet been said, or said with enough emphasis, is that power is also existential; it defines what it is to be human: "Every act, every condition, indeed, even the simple fact of existing is directly or indirectly linked to the conscious exercise and enjoyment of power."[124] Human power is not, despite the scientific preemptions of business writers, only or even mainly a natural phenomenon. It is not only or mainly a force of energy or a cause or effect. And thus it is not only to judge by its agency or effectiveness. In addition, human power expresses initiative and purpose. Its defining quality is freedom, which by definition lies beyond deterministic nature.[125] Thus human power is to be judged by its rightness and goodness.

The good of power rests upon its authority. Questions abound: What is this authority? Where does it come from? And how does it define the use and limits of power? Answers cannot be found in scientific thinking that distinguishes power from the good by sundering fact (what is) from value (what ought to be). Such thinking makes power its own authority and invites the jeopardy of power without scruple. Instead, answers must be found in thinking that reaches beyond nature to the divine. In its etymology, "authority" is a theological idea; that is, an idea about God. The word derives both from the Latin *auctoritas* meaning authorship and *augere* meaning augmentation. Authority is directly connected to the authorship of society. In antiquity those invested with authority were regarded as having the ability to interpret and/or augment the will of the founder.[126] In the Judeo-Christian tradition of the West, the founder and author of all creation is the God of revelation, the one to whom moral truth (the knowledge of good and evil) is uniquely known.[127] According to this tradition, which shares its theological premise with other of the world's great moral traditions, the human right to power begins in God's love, with his relinquishing to humankind some of his creative power. The human responsibility for power is to return God's love by enlarging and extending His creative will. Today, even if they are not aware of it, those invested with authority retain this right and responsibility to act on behalf of the author of authors, to create and get things done in the world.

In the Judeo-Christian tradition, the divine founding of man's power is confirmed at the beginning of the Old Testament, in chapter 1 of the Book of Genesis, in connection with man's destination.

> And God said, Let us make man, wearing our own image and likeness; let us put him in command of the fishes in the sea, and all that flies through the air, and the cattle, and the whole earth, and all the creeping things that move on the earth. So God made man in his own image, made in the image of God. Man and woman both he created them. And God pronounces his blessing on them, Increase and multiply and fill the earth, and make it yours; take command of the fishes in the sea, and all that flies through the air, and all the living things that move on the earth.[128]

The meaning of revelation for understanding power is neatly summarized by Romano Guardini, who finds echoed throughout the theology of the Old and New Testaments the idea that "man was given power over nature and over his own life, power that imparts both the right and the obligation to rule:"

> Man's natural God-likeness consists in this capacity for power, in his ability to use it and in his resultant lordship. Herein lies the essential vocation and worth of human existence—Scripture's answer to the question: Where does the ontological nature of power come from? Man cannot be human and, as a kind of addition to his humanity, exercise or fail to exercise power; the exercise of

power is essential to his humanity. To this end the Author of his existence determined him.[129]

To Lead is to Serve

Authority is the power of being in God. It is the sacred-order, literally "hierarchy" (from the Greek "hiera" meaning sacred and "arche" meaning order), in which we act in relation to God. This is not only a moral claim, but a factual one as well (for the good of human power cannot be separated from its truth). Human power takes its authority in relation to God, a fact that illuminates the often misunderstood Biblical injunction to "Render unto Caesar the things that are Caesar's, and unto God the things that are God's." This is not, as many seem to think, a command to divorce the secular from the sacred; to separate the private from the divine. To the contrary, it a command to put the two in order; to recognize that the power which is Caesar's comes to him and finds its proper scope in the authority of God. There is no true authority that does not trace back to God.

The key to authority is humility, which is not as imagined by Nietzsche or the existentialist philosophers under his sway, a decadent and unbecoming slavishness, but is its opposite, a virtue of supreme strength. The idea of human humility before the divine is a staple of religious thinking throughout history, especially in the monotheism of the West. The model of authority is Jesus Christ, in whom God's absolute and supreme power is realized in the humility of human form. In the person of Christ, God humbled himself before man. Again from Guardini:

> Jesus' whole existence is a translation of power into humility. Or to state it actively: into obedience to the will of the Father as it expresses itself in the situation of each moment...For the Son, obedience is nothing secondary or additional; it springs from the core of his being.[130]

The name of this humility of power is love; which as the life of Christ attests, conquers everything, including death itself. In and through love we come to:

> ...an existence whose power is unique in history, a power that knows no outer bounds, only those self-imposed from within: the bounds of the Father's will accepted freely, and so completely accepted that at every moment, in every situation, deep into the heart's initial impulse, that will's demands are effective.[131]

To exercise power with authority, therefore, is to serve God in humility. But how is this to be done? Whom and how shall we serve? Again the answer is Christ, who is the Word and the Way. Like Christ, one serves God when one serves the human person; the one made in God's image, the one aimed toward

God and who cannot rest except in God. Power is for spiritual health which, as Plato first described and St. Augustine later elaborated, depends on our relation to truth, to the good and the holy. Power that enlivens the human spirit by fostering these relations enjoys the authority of God and constitutes virtue. Power that sickens the human spirit by destroying these relations lacks authority and constitutes sin.

Thus to exercise power with authority in business or anywhere else is to help persons draw closer to God. Before all—before increasing market share, or reaching a quarterly sales goal, or returning an acceptable profit to shareholders—the business of business is the human person. To lead is thus to serve. This idea is no vague precept without indication, no "motherhood" without children. To the contrary, it is certain conduct with certain consequences visible in every human relation. A bare generation ago, Robert Greenleaf recognized the idea of a business leader exercising power in the service of persons as a viable concept of leadership. "A new moral principle," he wrote, "is emerging which holds that the only authority deserving one's allegiance is that which is freely and knowingly granted by the led to the leader in response to, and in proportion to, the clearly servant stature of the leader."[132] The "servant leader" serves first and leads second, "always accepts and empathizes, never rejects," sees love as an "unlimited liability," and sees that "the first order of business is to build a group of people who, under the influence of the institution, grow taller and become healthier, stronger, more autonomous."[133] The Christianity of the servant leader comes to light in Greenleaf's inspiration for the idea, the character Leo in Herman Hesse's novel, *Journey to the East*. At the end of that novel, as the narrator was to be inducted into the Order, he confronts a small transparent sculpture of the figure of Leo:

> I perceived that my image was in the process of adding to and flowing into Leo's, nourishing and strengthening it. It seemed that, in time...only one would remain: Leo. He must grow, I must disappear.[134]

In recent years, this notion of the servant leader has been become a popular strain of Evangelical Christian writing about business. Typical of the genre is *The Servant Leader* by Ken Blanchard and Phil Hodges which outlines a program of business leadership that supports and substantiates the ideas about authority and power above.[135] As the authors describe, the servant leader differs from the selfish leader in his/her exercise of power. Unlike the latter, the servant leader has his/her priorities in order (seeks the kingdom of God first and rejects anything that distracts from that end), embraces an eternal perspective on the here and now; seeks to lead for a higher purpose beyond success and significance, considers his/her position as being on loan and as a service, welcomes even negative feedback (is not ego defensive), plans for and grooms his/her successor (is not addicted to power), never asks anyone to do something they wouldn't do themselves, resists temptations of instant gratification, recognition, applause, and improper use and lust for power, is aware of and seeks to conquer the demon of pride, and keeps Jesus'instruction about plain and honest speech. In the concept of the servant leader in business we come to a fulsome image of power authorized by God, an image of what power in business can and should be.

With the sovereignty that God wishes human persons to exercise on His behalf we come to the folly of human being—namely that in freedom a person is able and apt to misuse power by putting it to private uses not God's. And indeed, this is what social scientists such as French & Raven, Bennis & Nanus, Pfeffer and Cialdini allow, without thinking much about it: that managers put power to private use. In effect, if not intent, they set the idea of power against the ideal of authority. By their lights power is to master the given; to exercise power in any given reality is to exercise control over it. But, as we have just seen, authority begins in and defers to a given; namely God who is author of every human reality. Whereas, for the social scientists, power means being able to employ force of one kind or another to coerce reality to its designs, authority calls upon the truth of God's creation to invite the freely chosen obedience of those over whom it rules. Indeed, for the social scientists, power that rests on free obedience is not true power because, by definition, that which is freely given is not mastered or controlled and could be withheld as freely as it is given. Again, to recall Pfeffer above, power is the ability to "get people to do things they would not otherwise do." Where authority sets limits on power; power seeks to overcome all limits, including especially those of authority.

In a fundamental sense the social science idea of power is nihilistic in that it rests upon the assumption that there is no God to whom power is accountable and no law to which it must submit. And with no God to answer, this power has no bounds to keep it from becoming totalitarian. As theologian Joyce Little points out:

> ...only authority can set limits of political power, because only authority in the realm of history confronts us with a reality larger than ourselves to which we are called to give our assent and scope. Such authority is always religious in nature, because the reality to which it bears witness is never of our making and always transcends us.[136]

By its nihilism, social science opens a door to the peril of management power without a governing ethic. According to Guardini, "power has come to be exercised in a manner that is not ethically determined; the most telling expression of this is the anonymous business corporation."[137] It is a peril known since antiquity; that of tyranny opposed to authority. Where an authority accepts power as a right and responsibility granted by an author greater than him/herself, a tyrant seizes power by and for him/herself. "Tyranny," wrote G.K. Chesterton, "means too little authority, not too much."[138] And, moreover, such power is no good even for its holder. According to Plato, the tyrant who did not revere the gods and did not respect the law was a forlorn and doomed figure. We say today that power corrupts and that absolute power corrupts absolutely. Confirms Guardini: "Nothing corrupts purity of character and the lofty qualities of the soul more than power. To wield power that is neither determined by moral responsibility nor curbed by respect for the person results in the destruction of all that is human in the wielder himself."[139] Power sundered from God is a cataclysm for man, both for his society and for himself.

Puzzles Resolved

The two puzzles of power can now be resolved in principle and, one hopes, in the conduct of our lives. In the first place we see both the truth and error in our ambivalence about power; that we are both right and wrong to fear the power by which we get things done in the world. On the one hand, our fear is founded in our wont to exercise power without authority and thereby endanger others and ourselves. Ours is the uneasiness examined by J.R.R. Tolkien in his modern classic, *The Lord of the Rings,* in which the central character, Frodo, embarks upon a hero's journey of faithful obedience to destroy the Ring of Power created by the Dark Lord Sauron—the "one ring to rule them all"—all the while tormented by its allure and by the importunities of his incorrigible companion, Sméagol. Central to Tolkien's meditation on power, and to our own, is the implacable truth that power is dangerous to us except as it is subject to the authority of God. On the other hand, our fear is also an error in that our true worry is not with power itself but with ourselves. Power, after all, is the energy and means of our lives; it is how we make our way in the world. Thus if we fear power it is because we fear ourselves. From ageless experience we know that we are wont to usurp God's authority and put power to ends of our choosing not his. And from this experience we know that we are apt thereby to destroy the society of those we love and destroy ourselves. The truth in God, however, is that there is nothing ambivalent about power. Power is God's pure gift of love to us, by which He granted us the right and responsibility of dominion in the world. Power is all to the good if we make straight our path to Him.

Second, and related, between the "toughest bosses" and the "humble and resolved leaders" we see why we loathe the one and laud the other. In such feelings we become aware of that inner voice that was there all along and that is who we are. In particular we heed that vague disconcertment in the thinking of reflective social scientists such as Kanter and Gardiner who pause at the idea that power is a morally neutral instrument of self-interest only. And at the same time we heed that call of our heart to love God and our neighbor as our self. In the Christian tradition, such intimations of the soul call to mind the exhortation of the Lord's Prayer, "Thy will be done," which we see not only as our hope but as the truth of our being. We are His servants and we are to obey His commands. This is the law of human power authorized by God; the moral law revealed by the great theological traditions of the world; the law within which we realize our right and responsibility of dominion in the world. This is "law" in both senses of the word; it is a truth about what we are (a law of human being) and it is a truth about how we must act (a law of right conduct). Our power belongs under God's authority.

Chapter 5

Business and the Human Person

In the broad terms that most of us speak in most of the time, it is almost too easy to criticize business. Viewed in the abstract, as an instrument of commerce rather than as human persons making lives for themselves, business is an off-putting affair. According to the "shareholder-value model" that dominates thinking about business in universities today and now sets the agenda for business in the wider culture, a business is a financial entity composed of resources, including employees who are "human resources," to be used to maximize the wealth of its owners.[140] Proclaimed today by students of economics and finance, this idea of business was anticipated and encapsulated years ago by Alfred P. Sloan, architect and executive of the General Motors Corporation, who opined that: "The business of business is business." This cool pragmatism has been taken by many to be the cardinal virtue of business. "It's nothing personal," we say, "it's just business." Business has become the conscienceless idea of "never mind." Never mind the plight of workers—they are their own contractors, free to come and go as they please. Never mind the common good of society—that is for government to decide. And never mind "corporate social responsibility"—that's just a "guilt trip" to coerce regrets business can not have.[141] Viewed in the abstract, as an instrument of economic interest, business is an ambivalent proposition at best.

Certainly business is no ambivalence in the literary imagination. In the caricature drawn by writers, business is a devil's bargain—wealth and amenity today for the soul in eternity. Its stock figures are the likes of Charles Dickens' Scrooge, a man estranged from love and life by a hard and flinty avarice, and Sinclair Lewis' Babbitt, a man no less estranged from love and life by a soft and needy middle class lifestyle.[142] These figures of greed and vacuity are real--truth is no stranger to fiction. Today's Scrooges are the "Barbarians at the Gate" of Wall Street and the "Smartest Guys in the Room" on the power trading floor at the Enron Corporation.[143] Today's Babbitts are denizens of the "Moral Mazes in the World of Corporate Managers" and, more generally, of America's pervading "Culture of Narcissism."[144]

A Bad Rap

Whatever their grain of truth such easy charges against business are a bad rap. They are founded upon misleading abstractions. The shareholder-value model of business is just that, a model, not the reality. And of course literary imagination is just that, imagination, not the whole truth. It is not business per se that gets us into trouble, but our thinking about business that gets us into trouble.

Our thinking about business falters for its conceit of truth. We fail to remember that our ideas about business are just that, "our ideas," and thus inherently partial and provisional. We fail to see that while an idea like the shareholder value model conveys a truth—namely that business is an economic enterprise to manage for the wealth of its owners—it also conveys a lie—namely that people are assets to deploy on behalf of owners. The latter is "wrong" in both senses of the word—it is factually wrong in that persons are more than material assets of a business, they are supernatural beings, children of God; and it is morally wrong in that it is an injustice to treat them as the former when they are the latter.[145] In a word, we get ourselves wrong. While we can think objectively about the things of the natural world that we can experience, we cannot think objectively about ourselves because we are not things of the same kind and we cannot experience ourselves in the same way. In fact, we are not things of the natural world at all, but are beings in the supernatural realm of God. Thus, while we can think objectively about every thing in nature, we cannot think that way about ourselves.[146] Being above nature—being literally "super-natural"—we are beyond our own estimate.[147]

Thus when we think about ourselves in the naturalistic and often scientific terms used in business today we do so at our peril. To keep hold of our human being we must reach beyond the usual business vernacular to God. We must accept in faith what He has revealed about us. With Pope John Paul II we must see that "Revelation has set within history a point of reference which cannot be ignored if the mystery of human life is to be known."[148] And more generally, and again with the Pope, we must see that our self understanding requires both faith and reason:

> Faith and reason are like two wings on which the human spirit rises to the contemplation of truth; and God has placed in the human heart a desire to know the truth—in a word, to know himself—so that, by knowing and loving God, men and women may also come to the fullness of truth about themselves.[149]

Looking to faith, we must find the reference points for understanding ourselves, the truths within which our thinking about business can be put in proper context. And looking to faith, we must augment our thinking about such things as the shareholder value model to acknowledge truths of the human person that originate outside the natural world of economics, in our being in God.

The question therefore is not whether we should use God's gift of reason in thinking about business. The question is not even whether in doing so we should use a tool such as the shareholder-value model. Indeed, we must think every thought and use every tool to make the most of business as a means to our dominion of the earth that God created for us. Rather, the question is *how* we should use God's gift of reason in thinking about business. To what end should our reason be put? To rephrase the question in the terms of Alfred P. Sloan, what should be the business of business? This ethical question is answered distinctively and decisively by the Catholic Church in what in recent decades, and particularly during the Pontificate of John Paul II, has come to be called her *Social Tradition.* In what follows I draw upon this tradition to suggest that the business of business—its weight and glory—is the human person. With the Church, I describe the weight of business in terms of eight principles that honor the dignity of the person in God. And with Catholic theologian and business writer Michael Novak, I describe the glory of business in terms of three cardinal virtues of business that help bring the person to God. I conclude with a confirming word from one of our greatest students of business, Mary Parker Follett.

To Make a Living

The business of business is to know, not in the cold abstractions of shareholder-value and not in the harsh light of literary examination, but in the warm flesh-and-blood of our personal lives and in the revelatory light of faith. The ethic of business is revealed in the nearness of human work that is personal and material, not in the distance of reason that is abstract precisely in that it has detached itself from both. Business is a matter of heart.

Nearly everyone speaks of work as a means to "make a living." But what does this mean? Is this a figure of speech that means "to make a buck" (to invoke another figure of speech)? Or is this a declaration of something much greater; namely, "to make a life"? According to faith we make a life by incarnation—literally by embodying God. To live is to be in God in body and mind. To live is to be in Christ who is "The Word" and "The Way." According to faith, the God of creation "spoke our being" in two ways—He named us His son, Adam, as the one in His image who shares in His power of naming and knowing; and He created us in love, as male and female in one flesh, as one who shares in His power to create life in love. Thus we incarnate God in two ways. We are a *person*, literally 'of son' to God. As such we are to answer and serve His will for us by following His commandments. And we are *man and woman in one flesh*, an embodiment of His creative will in love, especially in nuptial union from which we create new life. As such we are to extend His love in and through our love of others. Thus our human being is personal (a son-ship to God) and material (an embodiment of God).

In the person of Jesus Christ, carpenter of Bethlehem, we learn that one important arena in which we may incarnate God is work. Recounting the thought of Pope John Paul II in his encyclical on work, *Laborem Exercens*, Jean-Yves Calvez and Michael J. Naughton explain:

> Because they have been made in God's image, all people have been given the command, which is both a right and a duty, to subdue the earth. He defines the expression "subdue the earth" as a human activity that discovers all the resources the earth provides so as to use them for people to develop, not simply to maximize capital returns or to balance individual interests. It is only through work that people can tap the richness creation has to offer, and it is through organizations that this work is carried out most effectively.[150]

Thus we come into our humanity at work, and indeed everywhere else, when we come into the truth of our creation by God. As John Paul II described in a later encyclical about economic life, *Centesimus Annus*, without this realization we are lost to our own humanity:

> When man does not recognize in himself and in others the value and grandeur of the human person, he effectively deprives himself of the possibility of benefiting from his humanity and of entering into that relationship of solidarity and communion with others for which God created him.[151]

With the idea of divine incarnation we know what it means to make a living. It is to make a life in God. This reverses the usual understanding of the relationship between man and work. Too often it is supposed that man is for work; that he is an instrument of shareholder interests; and that he is responsible to these interests. The truth is to the contrary, that work is for man; that man has the right to be in God in and through the circumstances of work; and that business has the responsibility to honor this right. In a word, business is responsible for the divine lives of those in its employ. In a sharper word, the business of business is the human person. In allowing this much, and it is everything, we realize that business is not merely material and worldly; it is also spiritual and other-worldly. To serve its true purpose, the purpose that justifies its esteem in society, business must provide for the divine being of all whose lives it touches. This is something it cannot do if it reduces the person to an instrument of shareholder ambition.[152] Speaking to business on behalf of the human person, the Church reminds us that:

> Man cannot give himself to a purely human plan for reality, to an abstract ideal or to a false utopia. As a person, he can give himself to another person or to

> other persons, and ultimately to God, who is the author of his being and who alone can fully accept his gift.[153]

Unfortunately, as Calvez and Naughton point out, too often business does not allow people the opportunity and room to "make a life" in this way, but to the contrary alienates them by treating them as means rather than as ends.[154] As Pope John Paul II explains, "the concept of alienation needs to be led back to the Christian vision of reality, by recognizing in alienation a reversal of means and ends."[155]

What is more, in the idea of divine incarnation we understand what it means to "make a buck." We make money to provide for ourselves and others so that we may fulfill our vocation in God. Odd as it sounds, the work is not for the money, the money is for the work. We do not work for bread alone or indeed for bread at all. Sustained by bread we are able to fulfill one of our most important vocations, to be and grow in God.

The Weight and the Glory

Thus the business of business is not only or mainly to maximize shareholder wealth. It is more essentially to help persons make lives by creating conditions under which they can grow and develop in relationship to God. To be sure, it is a struggle for business to reconcile its worldly values for entrepreneurship and capital risk with its other-worldly values for life and being in God. As described by Pope John Paul II, business can and must not take a stand *against* making a profit, which is important and necessary for its well-being. Instead, business can and must take a stand *for* making human lives, which is in the end far more important and necessary for us all. The needful trick is to put the first value in the context of the second. According to John Paul:

> The Church acknowledges the legitimate *role of profit* as an indication that a business is functioning well. When a firm makes a profit, this means that productive factors have been properly employed and corresponding human needs have been duly satisfied. But profitability is not the only indicator of a firm's condition. It is possible for the financial accounts to be in order, and yet for the people—who make up the firm's most valuable asset—to be humiliated and their dignity offended. Besides being morally inadmissible, this will eventually have negative repercussions on the firm's economic efficiency. In fact, the purpose of the business firm is not simply to make a profit, but is to be found in its very existence as a *community of persons* who in various ways are endeavoring to satisfy their basic needs, and who form a particular group at the service of the whole of society. Profit is a regulator of the life of a business, but it is not the only one; *other human and moral factors* must also be considered which, in the long term, are at least equally important for the life of a business (italics in the original).[156]

As the business of business is to serve man, and the business of man is to serve God, the business of business is to serve God. This is the weight and glory of business;[157] its solemn responsibility and its noble virtue. And this is the work-order for business administration. I close this chapter with a too brief survey of what the weight and glory of business might mean for those who would lead.

The Weight

Business is not alone in its obligation to honor man's being in God; it can and must look for help to the Church who embraces this obligation as her mission for the whole of humankind. This is not to suggest that business can pass its responsibility off to the Church (as a value the Church might take up on Sunday mornings, while business plies other values the rest of the week); to the contrary, it is to insist that business accept its responsibility in league with the Church. It is perhaps in business more than in any other activity that Christian conscience encounters the real world. And thus it is perhaps in business especially that man's being in God must be realized.

On its path to salvation, business can find help in the Social Doctrine of the Church, which is her wisdom for man "as he is involved in a complex network of relationships within modern societies."[158] According to Pope John Paul II: "[B]y its concern for man and by its interest in him and in the way he conducts himself in the world," the Church's social doctrine "belongs to the field of theology and particularly of moral theology. The theological dimension is needed both for interpreting and solving present day problems in human society."[159] Directed to the whole of man's life in society, this doctrine comprises a set of guidelines within which business can and must take its place within society. Only by fidelity to these guidelines can business meet its obligation to the person and to society. This is the weight of business.

The Church's social doctrine is a living body; its elementary principles support one another in aid of man's personal and social destiny in God. To this end, while each principle is necessary, only the collection is sufficient. And while each principle warrants a chapter of its own, it must suffice in the pages remaining to this chapter to lay them out as a group so to see in broad terms the Church's wisdom for business. As compiled in her *Compendium of the Social Doctrine of the Church*, these principles are:

1) *Meaning and Unity*. This first principle refers to the entire set, to insist the collection be appreciated in its "unity, interrelatedness, and articulation."[160] This is to recognize that man's being in God is unitary and is to encourage and protect in all its aspects. Thus while individual doctrines refer variously to the person, to society, and to relations between the two, it must not be forgotten that person and society define one another as parts of God's unitary creation. For business this means that its obligation to the person cannot be separated from its

obligation to society. The business of business is man, both in person and in society.

2) *The Principal of the Common Good.* According to this principle: "A society that wishes and intends to remain at the service of the human being at every level is a society that has the common good—the good of all people and of the whole person—as its primary goal."[161] For business this means that its economic activity take place within the limits of the moral order and more particularly within God's plan for humankind. "The fundamental finality of ...production," according to the Church, "is not the mere increase of products nor profit or control but rather the service of man, and indeed of the whole man with regard for the full range of his material needs and the demands of his intellectual, moral, spiritual, and religious life; this applies to every man whatsoever and to every group of men, of every race and of every part of the world."[162] By this principle, the good of self-interest, which is so enshrined in business thinking today, cannot be all, or even first. Individual goods, including that of shareholders, must find their place within the super-ordinate good of humankind.

3) *The Universal Destination of Goods.* This is the principle that each and every person "must have access to the level of well-being necessary for his full development."[163] This is actually a two-handed principle: on one hand it confirms the necessity of private property as the ground upon which persons can make lives for themselves; on the other hand it recognizes that the earth and its resources are God's gift to all humankind for all to share and enjoy. Thus while this idea substantiates an absolute right to property and capital, this right is not unlimited but is instead constrained by the no less important and no less absolute right that the goods of God's gift to man be shared. For business, as Jean-Yves Calvez and Michael J. Naughton explain in describing the thought of Pope John Paul, this principle has clear meaning for its concepts of property and capital:

> Consequently, any idea of an absolute right to property and capital, expressed through formulas of shareholder wealth maximization, or any idea of a corporate body as merely a nexus of competing interests is rejected, because it denies the significance of this human vocation to work and impedes persons' development in and from their work. Nevertheless, this principle of universal destination "does not deligitimize private property; instead it broadens the understanding and management of private property to embrace its indispensable social function, to the advantage of the common good and in particular the good of society's weakest members."[164]

4) *The Principle of Subsidiarity.* According to this principle, "every social activity ought of its very nature to furnish help to the members of the body social, and never destroy and absorb them."[165] For the social activity of business this means that "While the authority of the owner ought to be protected, no room can exist in...business for practices that deny the profound worth of the employees of the enterprise."[166] This principle thus opposes two tendencies of modern business, particularly in its most highly industrialized sectors. One is the ten-

dency in manufacturing to treat worker as objects, as factors of production to manage like any other. This denies workers worth as autonomous and independent-minded subjects who take part in the creative will of God. The other is the tendency to treat workers as means to ends rather than as ends themselves. This equates the value of workers with what they produce rather than with who they are. To recognize workers as ends in themselves means that "...the entire process of productive work ... must be adapted to the needs of the person and to his way of life, especially in respect to mothers of families, always with due regard for sex and age."[167] Among these needs are the material ones of personal and family sustenance, which means that workers must be paid not only a living wage, but for workers with families a family wage. Also among these needs are those of self-expression and self-development: "The opportunity...should be granted to workers to unfold their own abilities and personality through the performance of their work."[168]

5) *Participation.* This principle provides for "activities by means of which the citizen, either as an individual or in association with others, whether directly or through representation, contributes to the cultural, economic, political, and social life of the civil community to which he belongs."[169] This principle carries a strong message for business at odds with the emphasis today upon shareholder capitalism. According to the Church:

> In economic enterprises it is persons who are joined together, that is, free and independent human beings created in the image of God. Therefore, with attention to the functions of each—owners or employers, management or labor—and without doing harm to the necessary unity of management, the active sharing of all in the administration and profits of these enterprises in ways to be properly determined is to be promoted. Since more often, however, decisions concerning economic and social conditions, on which the future lot of the workers and of their children depends, are made not within the business itself but by institutions on a higher level, the workers themselves should have a share also in determining these conditions—in person or through freely elected delegates.[170]

6) *The Principle of Solidarity.* This principle recognizes "the intrinsic social nature of the human person, the equality of all in dignity and rights, and the common path of individuals and peoples toward an ever more committed unity."[171] In a word, there is a unity of unities to which all human enterprise must tend. For business this means acting on behalf of the whole of humankind by producing goods that are truly "goods," that add to rather than subtract from the life of persons and society. Questionable, therefore, are businesses that contribute to vice and dissipation (such as by fostering use of unhealthy drugs or pornography) or businesses that through aggressive advertising create empty or misplaced "needs" (such as by playing up insecurities about physical beauty or social status). For business this also means that it act in cooperation with others, including its competition. Thus, competition in business is not, as some say, a

Hobbesian "war of all against all;" but instead a spirited play in which all are safe and secure, a Durkheimian "struggle for existence with a mellow denouement."[172] Competitors are not prey to overwhelm by market power or predatory pricing, but are loyal adversaries to welcome as a test of one's mettle in the marketplace. Competition is not cooperation's opposite, but its sincerest form.

7) *The Fundamental Values of Social Life.* According to this principle, "all social values are inherent in the dignity of the human person, whose authentic development they foster. Essentially, these values are: truth, freedom, justice, love."[173] There can be no human dignity—no human person and no human society—without these values, which every person and society must therefore uphold. For business these values must underlie every activity and relationship. It could hardly be otherwise as these values are written upon the human heart. In fact these values are presupposed by most abstract thinking about business, including particularly the shareholder value model, which begins upon an assumption of "the market." As Nobel economist Kenneth Arrow observes,[174] modern economic theory rests upon an idea of the market that it cannot explain. This market, Arrow notes, rests upon such humane values as truth, freedom, justice, and love. Thus, behind the conduct called for by abstract theories of business, is a mundane reality of fundamental values for human dignity called for by God and propounded in faith by the Church.

8) *The Way of Love.* This final principle finds in love the "highest and universal criterion of the whole of social ethics. Among all paths, even those sought and taken in order to respond to the ever new forms of current social questions, the 'more excellent way' is that marked out by love."[175] True happiness "is not found in riches or well-being, in human fame or power, or in any human achievement...but in God alone, the source of every good and of all love."[176] This principle recognizes in the most general way possible what it is to be in God. As God is love, we are in God when we are in love. This love is a 'many splendored thing' that begins in God and extends to every human relation and to every corner of existence. Love is dynamism of division in unity and unity in division. In the moment of love comes the moment of play whereby people together create a social order. Play is the creative edge of love whereby come new divisions in unity and new unities in division. [177] And in the moment of play comes the moment of individuation whereby persons take their place in the life of the whole. Individuation is a fruit of play, the division in unity and unity in division that is the human person in society.[178] Thus love is the ground of all social life, including that of business of course.

The Glory

Although the weight of business is a heavy one, rarely carried well or far, and too often confirmed in the dropping, it is the glory of business and the lie in our too easy criticism of it. At its best, business is a glory of God. It is a noble calling to being in God that serves man's heart's desire.

Business glorifies God as it helps man to his incarnation; to his realization of God in becoming a person and to his embodiment of God in taking part in a union of male and female in one flesh. Far from the cold abstractions of the shareholder value model, the glory of business is in the concrete doings of real people making real lives together. Among the voices for this glory is theologian Michael Novak who insists upon an image of business as a vocation; as a conscious or unconscious calling of the human spirit to God. In business he finds three cardinal virtues in whose exercise man comes to be in God: creativity, building community, and practical realism.[179] About the first, creativity, he writes:

> At the very heart of capitalism...is the creative habit of enterprise. Enterprise is, in its first moment, the inclination to notice, the habit of discerning, the tendency to discover what other people don't yet see. It is also the capacity to act on insight, so as to bring into reality things not before seen. It is the ability to foresee both the needs of others and the combinations of productive factors most adapted to satisfying those needs. This habit of intellect constitutes an important source of wealth in modern society.[180]

This virtue of creativity, which is the primary source of wealth and the engine of man's successful dominion of the earth, is man's imaging of God. By his creativity, man "participates from afar in the source of all knowledge, the Creator. Sharing in God's creativity...the principal resource of humans is their own inventiveness. Their intelligence enables them to discover the earth's productive potential..."[181]

About the second virtue, building community, Novak begins with the truism that capitalism is not about the individual, but is about "a creative form of community":

> In a word, businesspeople are constantly on all sides, involved in building community. Immediately at hand, in their own firm, they must build a community of work. A great deal depends on the level of creativity, teamwork, and high morale a firms' leaders can inspire.[182]

This virtue of building community, according to Novak, "throws a practical light" on a divine truth about the human person which faith affirms, a truth which again is a sign of man's imaging of God:

> That truth is this: *the Creator made the human person to work in community and to cooperate freely with other persons, for the sake of other persons* (italics in original).[183]

And finally, about the third virtue of business, practical realism, Novak traces a surprising connection between an alert and hard-nosed business practice and Providence. Comparing businesspeople to athletes and professional warriors, he notes in common a state of life given to peril which leads them to "be unusually aware of how many facets of reality are not under their control, how dependent they are on such factors, and the great difference between being smiled on—or frowned on—by Providence."[184] Whereas one might expect the practical realism of businesspeople to be far from faith, Novak finds in it an intimation of incarnation, of God in action. For this, many in business feel blessed—as if "God had shed His grace on thee"—so much so that "Those whose efforts to better the human community mark them as creators, made in the image of their Creator, develop a mental habit in which prayer seems to accord with the natural law itself—and even with the law of grace."[185]

Although founded upon the concrete actions of real persons in community, these virtues of business do not oppose the abstract value of making a profit or for that matter the use of rational techniques aimed at profit (such as those that might derive from the shareholder value model). Quite the contrary, these virtues promote the value of making money, which can be seen as a secondary virtue and glory of business. These virtues are the context within which exigencies of profit can be interpreted and appreciated. In these virtues we see that business is not only or mainly an exercise of economic rationality, but is truly an art of divine reach. Indeed, in view of its complexity, its human dimensions, and its premium on intuition and judgment, business might well be the practical art *par excellence*. Within this art, economic rationality is a tool like any other; its value and good are not intrinsic but depend upon how it is used. When it helps bring man to God it is a tool to the good and there is virtue in its use. When it diverts man from God it is an instrument of sin and there is evil in its use. Business is the worldly art of using all available tools for the glory that is God.

A Final Word

At chapter's end we recall the needful marriage of reason and faith. The Church honors her mission by advocating for that divine revelation that sets the reference points within which business can reason its way to salvation. In her Pastoral Constitution of Vatican II, *Gaudium et Spes*, the Church states that "In the economic and social realms...the dignity and complete vocation of the human person and the welfare of society as a whole are to be respected and promoted. For man is the source, the center, and the purpose of all social life." These reference points of person and society are the ultimate purposes that have guided the most acute students of business administration. Here, in a word from perhaps the greatest of these, Mary Parker Follett, we come to a fitting end:

> The leader releases energy, unites energies, and all with the object not only of carrying out a purpose, but of creating further and larger purposes. And I do not mean here by larger purposes mergers or more branches; I speak of larger in the qualitative rather than the quantitative sense. I mean purposes which will include more of those fundamental values for which most of us agree we are really living.[186]

Chapter 6

Christmas Thoughts on Business Education

> *"But you were always a good man of business, Jacob," faltered Scrooge, who now began to apply this to himself.*
> *"Business!" cried the Ghost, wringing its hands again. "Mankind was my business. The common welfare was my business; charity, mercy, forbearance, and benevolence, were all my business. The dealings of my trade were but a drop in the water in the comprehensive ocean of my business!"*[187]

How did we get to this dark place in business today? To this place of colossal accounting scandal (e.g., Enron, WorldCom, Adelphia, Tyco, Global Crossing, Arthur Andersen), stock and hedge fund manipulation (e.g., Bearing Point, ImClone), looting of pension funds, after-hours trading by financial services companies, crass exploitation of vanity (a $6 billion/yr cosmetic industry) and vice (a $15 billion/yr pornography industry), a coarse business culture of CEO celebrity, materialism, and style over substance, back-dated stock options, and obscene levels of executive pay and privilege? How did we get to this place of suspicion and broken trust in the business profession? When a recent Gallup Poll asked Americans to rank the honesty and ethics of 23 professions, they ranked the business professions in the bottom third, giving each more negative than positive scores. Business executives ranked 15th, stockbrokers ranked 17th, insurance salesmen ranked 20th, HMO managers ranked 21st, advertising practitioners ranked 22nd, and car salesmen ranked last at 23rd.[188]

It is said that the road to hell is paved with good intentions. A more illuminating way to say the same thing is to note, with C.S. Lewis,[189] that secondary goods pursued as if they are the primary good, become no goods at all. In the hell-bound lament of the ghost of Jacob Marley above, the lament of putting the good of a business trade ahead of the good of mankind, Charles Dickens telegraphs the moral of his 19th century classic *A Christmas Carol.* It is a moral for business education today.

This chapter is about the goods pursued in schools of business administration, in the United States especially, but all around the world as well. I argue that, without meaning to, business schools convey goods that work against the profession they serve. By putting secondary goods of the trade—in particular, the goods of the corporation, its shareholders, and managers themselves—before the primary good of business, they undermine all good and invite the hell of Marley's ghost: "The whole time … no rest, no peace. Incessant torture of remorse" (p. 23). Put plainly, if somewhat harshly, I suggest that business schools today offer students what amounts to a "bill-of-goods". And put plainly, if somewhat hopefully, I suggest, with Dickens, that business schools can and must do better.

But I am getting ahead of the story. This chapter unfolds as follows. I begin with the primary good of business; with the good that brings order to the many and varied secondary goods of business practice. This good, I find, is nothing other than the supreme good of a person—the *summum bonum.* This is the good of one's creative being; what the Catholic Church and the other great faith traditions of the world think of as his or her being-in-God. With Dickens, and with Michael Novak and Dennis Bakke today,[190] I see that business should and can be a sacred and redeeming calling, a 'vocation' in God. In view of this *summum bonum*, I then examine the goods that business schools today encourage in students. I find that while these goods have their place, when taken alone, apart from the *summum bonum*, they lead away from the true good of a person and the true good of business. I close the chapter with a few Christmas thoughts about how business schools might answer the calling of business life and thereby restore dignity to the people and organizations they serve.

The *Summum Bonum*

The good of business education is the good of humankind. Business does not exist apart from human life, but ranks among its most important activities and concerns. Business is limb to the tree of human life; it supports and is supported by the whole.

The good of humankind is to find in its essence, in the fundamental principle of human life. As G.E.M. Anscombe points out, for every kind of thing there is a "primary principle" or "soul"; a determinate form that it takes (or assumes as it grows and develops) and that comprises its good.[191] There is thus a water principle, a rose principle, a dog principle, and a human principle. For inanimate things, this principle or soul is that of matter. For the thing we call water, for example, it can be thought of as one matter scattered all over the world. Its good is the integrity of its physical being (its atoms and/or molecules). For the things we call plants and animals, this principle or soul is that of a bodily life. A rose or a dog is an organism that grows and develops in a characteristic way from seed to senescence. It's "rose-ness" or "dog-ness" is fully canvassed and fully distinguished by its organism. Its good is the good of its bodily life. And for the thing we call human this principle or soul is the creative mind—the capacity of insight, imagination, compassion, analysis, play, logic, and invention. Humans live as humans when they think and feel (when *Homo sapiens*) and perhaps never more than when they play (when *Homo ludens*).[192] A human person's creative mind reaches beyond the body—it is spirit beyond matter. Philosophers such as Anscombe describe mind as a "subsistent immaterial being". Theologians identify mind with God, the subsistent immaterial Creator of all things. A person is not merely an animal life, but a divinely ordained being, a child of God. His or her good, therefore, is uniquely bound up with God.

The good of humankind appears both in the person and in society. It is an axiom of most theologies, and certainly of Christianity, that the human person is defined by his/her being in God, by his/her vocation in God's creation.[193] In this divine aspect the person is prior to worldly things, prior to time and space, prior even to the material body. One's supreme good, his/her *summum bonum*, therefore, is his or her being in God. It is a good realized only imperfectly in this life, depending on how the person plays his or her part.

At the same time that man or woman is person he or she is part of the society of humankind. The unity humankind is no poet's dream, or misanthrope's nightmare; it is the communal form of God's creation. The original form and template for society is the family, beginning with the nuptial union of man and woman in one flesh. This bodily realization of the person in society is also an image of God, also a realization of man's being in God. One's good, therefore, finds its social dimension in the nuptial union,[194] and is elaborated in the myriad forms of social life which grow upon that original union.[195] The divinely creative being of the person is enlarged and completed by the divinely creative being of society. Figures of divine society are to find in the myriad groups that man makes—of tribe, nation, culture, community, and business. These last are more or less true to a person's being in God and thus more or less true to his or her *summum bonum*.

Person and society thus are of a piece; each implies the other; the two together comprise the creative soul of humankind. The connection between them is concrete and familiar in the family, in which persons are born, grow, and develop in its love and life. But the connection between them appears as well on the greater scale of human culture, as for example in the phenomenon of language, in which persons grow and develop in its love and life.[196] Indeed, all that is creative—all that is distinctively human—is twofold in this way; belonging both to the person and to society.[197] One comes into his or her person in communion with others. This is a further aspect of his or her supreme good, that his or her being as person in God is only realized in society with others.

Returning to business, Timothy Fort calls the business corporation a "mediating institution" to recognize that it is a figure and expression of the divine in man.[198] Where the corporation serves humankind's divine person and divine society, it enjoys the good it brings to both. Where it fails to do so, it suffers the evil it brings to both. The good of business, therefore, is its being in God. It is the good summarized by Saint Augustine: "You have made us for yourself, O Lord, and our hearts are restless until they rest in you" (PL 32, 661).[199]

The "Goods" of Business Education

> *Oh! but he was a tight-fisted hand at the grindstone, Scrooge! a squeezing, wrenching, grasping, scraping, clutching, covetous old sinner! Hard and sharp as flint, from which no steel had ever struck out generous fire; secret and self-contained, and solitary as an oyster. The cold within him froze his old features, nipped his pointed nose, shriveled his cheek, stiffened his gait; made his eyes red, his thin lips blue and spoke out shrewdly in his grating voice. A frosty rime was on his head, and on his eyebrows, and his wiry chin. He carried his own low temperature always about with him; he iced his office in the dog-days; and didn't thaw it one degree at Christmas.*[200]

Business education—like every professional education—is moral in the precise sense that it is about how to act in the world. It is to judge by its good and bad, by its right and wrong. Whose interests does business education serve—owners, managers, employees, stakeholders, communities, all of the above? What defines good management—profit, market share, quality products, fair prices, stock value, employee well-being, return to society, environmental stewardship? What responsibility does business have to the person? What responsibility does it have to society? What are the limits of fair competition? Should work be fit to the worker, or should the worker be fit to the work? What is a fair wage? What is a fair distribution of profits among owners, managers, and workers? What obligations does business have to governments? What responsibility does business have to the natural environment? Such questions—and many more could be added—are moral questions.

The grounds for answering such moral questions are less settled today than ever before. Tectonic shifts in American capitalism—in economic base from farming to manufacturing to information services; in markets from local communities to regions to nations to the whole of the globe; in financing from elite financiers, to commercial banks, to markets of every imaginable kind[201]—have shaken the moral foundations of American business. It used to be simpler. As described by Max Weber, American capitalism arose and prospered in the 18th and 19th centuries within a generally agreed-upon—if not always faithfully lived—Protestant Christian ethic that saw success in a worldly calling as a sign of election by God and that put stock in hard-work, personal asceticism, and capital investment.[202] According to this ethic, business was a patrimony (a familial form, a worldly church) and its profit was a spiritual good before God. Its paradigm was the small family business. Although remnants of these values were still to find late into the 20th century, they have been worn to threads by the tectonic shifts just noted. Election by God has become an irrelevance amidst diversions of surplus wealth, consumerism, celebrity culture, opportunistic investment, and bureaucratic organization. More and more we have created the culture of narcissism described by Christopher Lasch—an amoral world of selfishness, concern for style over substance, easy offense, sexual license, entitlement, emotional immaturity, fascination with success and fame, and lack of concern for others including children.[203] We have created a business ethic which, as detailed by Robert Jackall:

> ... breaks apart substance from appearances, action from responsibility, and language from meaning. Most important, it breaks apart the older connection between the meaning of work and salvation. In the bureaucratic world, one's success, one's sign of election, no longer depends on one's own efforts and on an inscrutable God but on the capriciousness of one's superiors and the market; and one achieves economic salvation to the extent that one pleases and submits to one's employer and meets the exigencies of an impersonal market.[204]

Although business schools have been around for better than 100 years,[205] business education only came to flower in the late 1950's and early 1960's. As reported by Jeffrey Pfeffer and Caroline Fong, whereas only 3,200 Master of Business Administration (MBA) degrees were awarded in the United States in 1955-56, that number had mushroomed to over 102,000 in 1997-98.[206] According to *U.S. News and World Report*, by 2001, 1,292 schools (92% of accredited colleges and universities in the US) offered an undergraduate business major, the most popular major in the country, by far. Also during this period, beginning in the late 1950's, business schools took a new form by converting themselves from "trade schools" (from weak cousins of prestigious university departments of arts and sciences) to scientifically-oriented research institutions (to equal partners with these other university departments).[207] In the perspective of history, it now seems possible that these two facts are connected; that business education prospered as it offered a scientific alternative to the crumbling Christian foundations of business, something it was able to do by capitalizing on the prestige of the university.

Business education today, particularly MBA education today, is almost entirely typical. A survey of MBA programs in the US and around the world finds an impressive uniformity in educational missions, course offerings, and degree requirements. MBA education is a fine example of what sociologists call a "social institution." Its ways and means are fit to a pattern. Some of this pattern comes from accreditation requirements of the *Association to Advance Collegiate Schools of Business* (AACSB). And some of this pattern comes from market pressures upon schools to show well in rankings of MBA programs by media such as *Business Week*, *The Wall Street Journal*, *The Economist*, and *U.S. News and World Report*. To succeed in these rankings schools must score well on a certain few criteria of student qualifications, student evaluations of programs, and assessments of schools by corporate recruiters. For chasing the same criteria, and for fear of falling behind competitors, business schools often choose what seems to be the "safe" course of imitating one another.

Goods in the Classroom

What does the MBA teach about the good of business? Certainly it does not teach the one true good of a person, his or her creative being in God. Indeed, one would have to look very hard to find mention of God anywhere in MBA education. Instead, the MBA teaches a great many other things that are taken to be goods because they are useful for the end of making money. Business is seen as an instrumentality, as a technical device or a machine. It does not matter so much what the machine does or how it does it (there are many ways to make a buck), it matters more that the machine run well and at a profit. The MBA teaches that business is essentially pragmatic, motivated by what works. This pragmatism is its own morality.

The focus of the MBA on instrumentalities begins at the beginning, with a required core curriculum that focuses both on fundamentals of business thinking (in courses such as micro and macro economics, financial accounting, strategy, and business statistics), and business practice (in courses such as finance, managerial accounting, marketing, operations management, and human resources management). The goods of the MBA core curriculum are the instrumentalities of its courses. The good of micro economics is to apply economic reasoning to managerial decision making. The good of accounting is to gather information about costs and prices to make efficient internal business decisions. The good of finance is accurate financial evaluation to make a profit under conditions of risk and uncertainty—and so on for the other business disciplines.

The focus on business instrumentalities, begun in the core, is extended and elaborated in the elective curriculum that follows. In its elective courses, the MBA describes business even more plainly as an exercise of technique. Strategy electives elaborate on environment analysis, competitive strategy, globalization, growth, and sustainable enterprise. Entrepreneurship electives add ideas of new venture creation, family business, and managing growth through new ventures. Marketing electives elaborate on brand management, distribution, market planning, consumer behavior, and new product management. Again, a similar account can be given for the other areas of business education.

Ironically, this bonfire of the instrumentalities is confirmed even in elective courses on business ethics where questions about the ends of business are often subordinated to students' own practical purposes. Here, for instance, is the catalog description of the business ethics elective course at one of the nation's leading business schools, a course typical of the genre:

> The goals of the course are to assist you in clarifying your values, to create awareness of the ethical issues that may arise in your career, and to provide you with a framework for moral decision-making. This framework will connect

> with your own moral intuitions, but will also assist you in providing "reasons" and "justifications" for your actions or beliefs, and not simply "opinions." We will consider ethical dilemmas you may face as a manager and help you determine what is a "right," "just," and "fair" result, and how to implement your decision in a manner that is politically feasible (i.e., What works in the real world? How will that decision affect my interests and my career?). We will also discuss the challenges involved in creating organizations that support ethical behavior. In addition, we address the broader issues of the appropriate roles and responsibilities of the corporation in society.[208]

This course is not concerned with moral truths, but with students' values. Students are not taught what is good, but are encouraged to decide the good for themselves. This course hedges the good in quotation marks–of what is "right", "just", and "fair"—thus to suggest the good has not one meaning, but several meanings, or perhaps no meaning. And this course offers "reasons" and "justifications" that "work in the real world." Its good is the practicality of one's own purposes.

Looking across the courses of the MBA one sees its cast of mind. Keeping with its technical focus, the MBA tends to the abstract and impersonal. This is true even in courses that rely on case studies, which are used to illustrate universal principles. Business is a story told of income, cash flow, assets, inventory, sales, receivables, debt, supply, demand, price, information, risk, probability, net present value, costs, efficiency, and profit. The story pits business against market forces and plays out in strategy, risk/return tradeoffs, decision-making under uncertainty, financial leveraging, budgeting, pricing, market segmentation, competition, and leadership. Business is a board game of pieces to manipulate and move for advantage.

Thus, by its focus on means rather than ends, and by its focus on the abstract and impersonal rather than the concrete and personal, business education conjures business as a technical and amoral exercise. The business of business is business. It takes its direction from the science of economics that says how to make money as effectively and efficiently as possible. This image does not trouble with the question of whether it is good to treat persons and groups as means rather than ends. This image is not disturbed by the typical accounting course that defines human labor as a variable cost, like other costs of production. And this image is not disturbed by the typical management course that defines people as "resources" (human resources) to be used for business ends. The word "manage" that appears everywhere in business education derives from the Latin root 'mand' for hand, as in manacle or manipulate, and is related to the French word "managere," the practice of training horses. To manage is to put resources to work for a purpose. Persons and groups are to deploy and manipulate to the same ends as raw materials, capital, and information.[209] About this education one could be forgiven for wondering what happened to the human; what happened to the person and community and love and God.

Misgivings

This chapter is hardly the first and certainly will not be the last to express misgivings about business education. There are gathering voices of doubt about the practical and moral value of business schools. For example, Pfeffer and Fong reviewed the evidence they could find to discover that "what little data there are suggest that business schools are not very effective: Neither possessing an MBA degree nor grades earned in courses correlate with career success, results that question the effectiveness of schools in preparing their students. And, there is little evidence that business school research is influential on management practice, calling into question the professional relevance of management scholarship."[210] The main function of business school, they suggest, is not to educate students, but to assure corporate recruiters a supply of applicants who are bright, hardworking, and already socialized to the ways and means of business.

Warren Bennis and James O'Toole also question the value of business schools, criticizing them for "failing to impart useful skills, failing to prepare leaders, and failing to instill norms of ethical behavior."[211] The fault, they argue, lies with a business curriculum predicated on "an inappropriate—and ultimately self-defeating—model of academic excellence."[212] They observe that in last several decades business schools have pushed for a model of science (larded with abstract economic analysis, statistical multiple regression and even laboratory psychology) that not only does not serve the needs of business practice but has driven out other more useful models of expertise. Business schools, Bennis and O'Toole warn, are "institutionalizing their own irrelevance"[213] by losing touch with managers' professional concern for practice. In this assessment the authors quote Thomas Lindsey, a former university provost at the University of Dallas:

> Business education in this country is devoted overwhelmingly to technical training. This is ironic, because even before Enron, studies showed that executives who fail—financially as well as morally—rarely do so from lack of expertise. Rather, they fail because they lack interpersonal skills and practical wisdom; what Aristotle called prudence. Aristotle taught that genuine leadership consisted in the ability to identify and serve the common good. To do so requires much more than technical training. It requires an education in moral reasoning, which must include history, philosophy, literature, theology, and logic.[214]

Such criticisms of business schools converge on the idea that business education is not enough about the problems managers face in acting for the good of business. By seeking academic legitimacy and moral sanction in science, business schools evade and exacerbate the moral challenges of the profession they serve. As Sumatra Ghoshal describes, the problem is not simply that the scientific theories taught in business school are useless for practice, but much worse, that "by propagating ideologically inspired amoral theories, business schools have actively freed their students from *any sense of moral responsibility*" (italics added).[215] According to Ghoshal:

> Management theories at present are overwhelmingly causal or functional in their modes of explanation. Ethics, or morality, however, are mental phenomena. As a result, they have had to be excluded from our theory, and from the practices that such theories have shaped. In other words, a precondition for making business studies a science as well as a consequence of the resulting belief in determinism has been the explicit denial of any role of moral or ethical considerations in the practice of management.[216]

If it is true, as critics say, that business schools do not improve the managerial acumen of their graduates and do not improve the organizations that employ their graduates, it is left to ask what good are they. In view of faults and failures that are supposed to be more recognizable by the day, how do business schools remain viable and how do they justify the monetary premiums they collect for their students and themselves? Might the answer lay in the economic changes noted earlier, particularly the opening of global markets, the transition from industrial to post-industrial economies, and the supplanting of stable and often humanly concerned corporations by volatile and often humanly indifferent financial markets? Might these changes have concentrated managers' attention upon the concerns of business owners at the expense of the concerns of other stakeholders such as employees, suppliers, distributors, society, and the natural environment? Could it be that business schools came into their own by providing managers both the tools and moral justification to address these concerns? And could it be more than a coincidence that business schools today deal mostly in formulae and management techniques to maximize shareholder wealth; formulae and techniques they justify as economic science?[217]

Finally, before leaving these criticisms of the MBA, it is well to note certain counter movements that have lately arisen within this education. Against the moral tide described above are scattered efforts to direct attention to goods beyond the merely instrumental, efforts that yearn for larger purposes, for transcendent meanings. This is to see in ideas that leadership is about making a difference, that the corporation has a responsibility to society, and that the student is a citizen. And this is to see in calls for stewardship of the natural environment (so-called "green management"), for solving global problems of economic disadvantage and poverty through "bottom-of-the-pyramid" business initiatives, and for a "positive organization studies" focused on authentic human relations, social vitality, personal virtues, and resilience. To yearn is to hope for what is not yet. To yearn is to call upon better angels.

First Things and Second Things

He was not alone, but sat by the side of a fair young girl in a mourning dress: in whose eyes there were tears, which sparkled in the light that shone out of the Ghost of Christmas Past.
"It matters little," she said softly. "To you, very little. Another idol has displaced me; and if it can cheer and comfort you in time to come, as I would have tried to do, I have no just cause to grieve."
What Idol has displaced you?" he rejoined.
"A golden one."
"This is the even-handed dealing of the world!" he said. "There is nothing on which it is so hard as poverty; and there is nothing it professes to condemn with such severity as the pursuit of wealth!"
"You fear the world too much," she answered gently. "All your other hopes have merged into the hope of being beyond the chance of its sordid reproach. I have seen your nobler aspirations fall off one by one, until the master-passion, Gain, engrosses you. Have I not?"[218]

The moral poverty of business education is simply understood. It is the poverty of not knowing the nature and source of the good; namely, man's creative being in God. It is the poverty of not knowing that all good serves this human being and that all evil opposes this human being. In this poverty, business education cannot tell which of its values are good and which of its values are evil. Its nobler aspirations fall to the master passion of gain.

Moral order begins in the distinction between the first thing and second things; between the primary good and secondary goods. As noted, man's primary good—his/her *summum bonum*—is the essential good of his/her being, the *telos* for which he/she was made.[219] This first and essential good is man's creative being in God; the good realized by taking part in God's creation. This good is not given by nature, but must be achieved in freedom against the long odds of man's sinfulness. As relayed in the Biblical story of Eden, man is a fallen being who must overcome sin to come into being with God. In contrast, man's secondary goods derive from the primary good. They are means to human being in God. Secondary goods bring man to God. Secondary evils take man from God. Many of the things widely valued in society today—wealth, luxury, status, and the rest—may not bring man to God and may not be goods, even if that is what they are called. And many of the things widely devalued in society today—poverty, pain, suffering, and the rest—may bring man to God and may be goods, even if that is not what they are called. Indeed, values and goods are not always or usually the same thing.

This is the moral order in which to judge the values of business education. We can ask, for example, does the value for business success, indicated by market share, profit, or stock price, serve the good of the person and the good of society? Can it do so? When does it do so? Or, does self-development, realized as leadership, full-engagement, or personal growth, serve the good of the person and the good of society? Can it do so? When does it do so? Such questions cannot be answered with a simple and automatic 'yes'. They are to answer in the event, in concern for the persons and society involved. Thus the value of making a profit could be a secondary good when it supports a business that provides people a living wage and opportunity to work creatively with others, but it is not a secondary good when it comes at the expense of these essentials. And thus the value of self-development could be a secondary good when it leads to creative being in God, but it is not a secondary good when it leads to selfishness apart from God. Thus the distinction between man's primary and secondary goods lights the way to a true ethic of business and thereby to a true education in business.

No Good Apart from the Primary Good

There are two important and related implications of the moral order of primary and secondary goods. One, developed in detail by MacIntyre,[220] is that failure to recognize the primary good results in the loss of all good. Again, what one accomplishes, what he or she thinks and does, are goods only in respect to the primary good that joins them in the whole of human life. Thus, when business education forsakes the primary good—when it trades in values that are not connected to one's being in God—it loses contact with the good. It becomes a kind of diversion, or worse a kind of hell. This loss of contact with the good is to see in the two telltale aspects of business education today: 1) its moral vacuity; and 2) its reliance upon an abstract and otherworldly economic reasoning.

The moral vacuity of business education consists in its unquestioned values. While this education correctly values such things as economic performance (e.g., costs, sales, profit, market share, customer loyalty), effective practice (e.g., leadership, innovation, technology, efficiency), and the students themselves (e.g., their energy, confidence, balance, growth, commitment, full-engagement), it does not ask if and how these values connect to man's primary good. For this reason, there is no telling when its values are truly goods and when they are instead expressions of selfishness or exploitation. Consider, for example, the value of maximizing shareholder wealth. When is this value a good? And when is this value an evil? Milton Friedman famously "answered" these questions by fiat, declaring shareholder wealth the one, only, and always good of business.[221] Edward Freeman demurred to argue that business has several stakeholders whose interests must be tallied to the good.[222] The debate between these views is unresolved.[223] We now know why; there is no resolving this or any moral question without a primary good.

Business education's loss of contact with the good is to see also in its reliance upon an abstract and otherworldly economics. This economics is a world unto itself, a world of its own means and ends. It is a world occupied not with human lives, not with human sensibilities and loves, but with impersonal markets grasped numerically and mulled logically.[224] This economics beguiles with mathematics and the idols of economic success. It is an example of what G.K.

Chesterton memorably described in another context—barren intellectualism, moonshine:

> Detached intellectualism is (in the exact sense of a popular phrase) all moonshine; for it is light without heat, and it is secondary light, reflected from a dead world. ... But the circle of the moon is as clear and unmistakable, as recurrent and inevitable, as the circle of Euclid on a blackboard. For the moon is utterly reasonable; and the moon is mother of lunatics and has given to them all her name.[225]

This impersonal and logical economics is lunacy precisely because it is out of touch with the mystery of one's being in God that keeps him or her sane. Again, as Chesterton notes, the mark of madness is the combination of logical completeness and spiritual contraction. "The madman is not the man who has lost his reason. The madman is the man who has lost everything except his reason."[226]

A Secondary Good Mistaken as the Primary Good Becomes No Good

A second implication of the moral order of primary and secondary goods is that a secondary good pursued for itself, apart from its connection to the primary good, results in the loss of that good. C.S. Lewis, who has expressed so many important things well, describes this implication as follows:

> The longer I looked into it the more I came to suspect that I was perceiving a universal law. *On cause mieux quand on ne dit pas Causons* ['One converses better when one does not say "Let us converse"']. The woman who makes a dog the centre of her life loses, in the end, not only her human usefulness and dignity but even the proper pleasure of dog-keeping. The man who makes alcohol his chief good loses not only his job but his palate and all power of enjoying the earlier (and only pleasurable) levels of intoxication. It is a glorious thing to feel for a moment or two that the whole meaning of the universe is summed up in one woman—glorious so long as other duties and pleasures keep tearing you away from her. But clear the decks and so arrange your life ... that you have nothing to do but contemplate her, and what happens? Of course this law has been discovered before, but it will stand re-discovery. It may be stated as follows: every preference of a small good to a great, or a partial good to a total good, involves the loss of the small or partial good for which the sacrifice was made.
>
> You can't get second things by putting them first, you can get second things only by putting first things first. From which it would follow that the question, 'What things are first?' is of concern not only to philosophers but to everyone.[227]

Without a first thing—a *summum bonum*—to organize and integrate values into a living whole, values can only clash with one another and work against the good. Without the first thing—the *summum bonum* that is man's creative being in God—values can only work at cross purposes to the good of the person and society. Where business education promotes values that do not put the first thing first, it frustrates those values. This is the lament of businesses that fail by giving too much attention to financial targets or too much attention to engineered efficiencies and not enough attention to the persons it asks to do the work and to the community it means to serve with a good product at a fair price.[228] And this is the morality tale of senior executives who see too late that a life devoted to personal success and wealth comes at the expense of a life of love with others in God. These are dangers of not putting first things first. More precisely and explicitly, these are dangers of putting other things before our creative being in God.

Of all these dangers, however, the most severe and cruel by far is that of putting one's self before God. Ever since Adam and Eve this has been our greatest temptation and therefore our most besetting sin. Two examples in business education serve the point. First, in the name of leadership development, students are often encouraged to seek the truth of leadership within themselves. Taken to its logical end—an end its teachers do not intend—this becomes an idea of the self as God; an idea, it must be said, that has inspired more than one tyranny in history—think of the brutal tyrannies of Stalin, Hitler, and Mao in world politics, or the petty tyrannies of Scrooge and Marley in business. Second, in the name of ethics training, students are often taught that ethics is a question of acting with integrity according to one's own values. The good is what one chooses it to be. This is an ethic without a *telos*, an ethic without design and without authority. This is an ethic of the sort argued by John Rawls that leaves each person free to pursue his/her own desires (provided that no harm is done to others).[229] Taken to its logical end—again an end its teachers do not intend—this becomes an idea of guiltless liberality; an idea that many blame for the moral chaos, decadence, and nihilism of Western culture today.[230] Behind this liberal ethic and behind the inner leadership above lies a value for an enlightened self, a self in possession of the great and good, a self before God, and, alas, a self assured of its own destruction.

Toward a Business Education in the Good

"Good Spirit," he pursued, as down upon the ground he fell before it. "Your nature intercedes for me and pities me. Assure me that I yet may change these shadows you have shown me by an altered life!"
The kind hand trembled.
"I will honour Christmas in my heart, and try to keep it all the year. I will live in the Past, the Present, and the Future. The Spirits of all Three shall strive within me. I will not shut out the lessons that they teach. Oh, tell me I may sponge away the writing on this stone!"[231]

> A man cannot think himself out of mental evil; for it is actually the organ of thought that has become diseased, ungovernable, and, as it were, independent. He can only be saved by will or faith.[232]

The great need of business education is to put its moral house in order by an act of will and faith. Business educators need to think differently about people and organizations, to see them in the light of the good which is the light of divine being. What Owen Barfield said about his field of psychology is true no less of the field of business education. It forgets the descent of the person from the divine. It thinks one's life is rooted in selfish energies, rather than in the inspiration of God. And it supposes that one's good lies in selfish experiences and acquisitions, rather than in relation to God.[233] A true business education must recognize that a person is higher than the natural; that he or she is supernatural. The idea of one's divine being changes everything and is the key to the good.

What will the required moral housecleaning mean for business education? In a word, it will mean great change. In the few words left to me in this chapter, I draw upon the argument so far to sketch two crucial changes that must come to business education to bring it to the good. It is but a start upon a positive program that will take all our creative energies and faith in God's grace to bring into being.

A True Idea of the Human Person

The first and most important change in business education must be that it begin upon a true idea of the human person, who is not what natural science says, a creature shaped by bodily needs, and who is not what social science says, a rational actor guided by self-interest. The human person is a divine but fallen being who comes to life with others in God. As Reinhold Niebuhr points out, man is distinctive among the creatures of the earth, not in physical power or prowess, and not even in superior reason or intellect, but in capacity for self-transcendence, in capacity for a relationship to God.[234] And, as Romano Guardini adds, man is "determined by the spirit; but the spirit is not 'nature'. The spirit lives and acts neither by historical nor by metaphysical necessity, but of its own impulse. It is free."[235] Consequently, "man does not belong exclusively to the world; rather, he stands on its borders, at once in the world yet outside it, integrated into it yet simultaneously dealing with it because he is directly related to God."[236]

To begin upon a true idea of man or woman, business education must face at least two facts that do not conform to its usual mode of economic thinking. One is that he or she is not an autonomous individual, but is a person in God. This is to say that the human person is not an indivisible unit walled off from others but is intimately involved with others in the life and love of God. And this is to say that man is not essentially selfish but is essentially compassionate and charitable. As a person, one cannot be described as the selfish "utility-maximizer" of economic lore, but must be described as the one made in the image of God, as the one who seeks to join with others in the life and love of God, and the one whose heart's desire is to please God. This person is infinitely greater and more important than a 'worker' or 'employee' or even a 'stakeholder', not to mention a 'fixed cost' or 'factor of production' or 'human resource'. To recognize this person is not to deny self-interest, but to see self-interest as directed to and bounded by interest in God. It is to see that people are not moved by abstract economic utilities but by a flesh and blood love of others in God. And to recognize this person is to begin to understand the responsibility of those who manage, for they are called to look after this person and thereby serve in the worldly ministry of God. As C.S. Lewis and so many others have pointed out, people are not things to manipulate and manage as pieces on a chessboard, but are children of God to be helped into relation with the Father.[237] Management is not about making a profit. It is about realizing the human person in the world.

A second fact about man or woman that does not conform to the usual mode of economic thinking in business education is that he or she is fallen. A human person is not only the one who, in freedom, pursues wants and desires; he or she is also the one who, in freedom, obeys or disobeys the law of his or her creation. The idea of the fall is that man's all-too-human being succumbs to the selfish evil of sin. Sin, according to Niebuhr, has both a religious and moral dimension: "The religious dimension of sin is man's rebellion against God, his effort to usurp the place of God. The moral and social dimension of sin is injustice. The ego which falsely makes itself the center of existence in its pride and will-to-power inevitably subordinates other life to its will and thus does injustice to other life."[238] This idea of sin is all but lost in the liberal ethic of business economics that identifies the good with what one desires instead of what God desires and that confuses one's economic power with God's moral authority. It is a casualty of the relativism and nihilism of modern secular culture.[239] Nevertheless, sin is a necessary element of moral order. For there to be good there must be evil, for there to be virtue there must be sin.

The *Summum Bonum*

A second and more directly practical change in business education must be that it begin with a clear understanding of the human person's *telos*, with a clear understanding of the primary good that is a person's heart's desire. This *telos*, as we've seen, is one's creative being in God. And this *telos*, as we've seen, defines all of one's derivative or secondary goods. With this *telos* in mind, business education must begin its every inquiry about management practice with two questions: Is this practice for the good of the person? And is this practice for the good of society?

Regarding the person, business education must ask and answer how its myriad values and ways bear upon the creative being of the person in God. This is not to ignore the usual business priorities for decreasing costs, increasing efficiency, increasing market share, and maximizing profits, but it is to see these priorities differently, as subordinate to the good of the person. It is to ask, for example, how management actions to achieve economic goals affect opportunities of workers to fulfill their divine vocation for creative work. Do management actions turn work into a dull routine, or put the worker under the control of a machine? Or, do they perhaps open up new possibilities for creative expression? The crucial lesson is that economic goals are not the ends of business, but means to the end that is the person in God. The task is to cultivate a management practice that reaches to the divine in every person.

Regarding society, business education must ask and answer no less how its values and ways bear upon the creative being of society in God. People take their place in society with others and just as the person demands respect as an image of God so too society demands respect as an image of God. Again this is not to ignore the usual business priorities, but again it is to see them differently, as subordinate to the good of society. It is to ask, for example, how management actions to achieve economic goals affect opportunities of workers to make a wage that can support their families and the community in which they live. Do management actions result in layoffs that devastate the family and community, or result in inadequate pay that works more slowly to the same end? Or do they perhaps expand the income pie for everyone by enlarging the market? Again the crucial lesson is that economic goals are not the ends of business, but means to the end that is society in God. And again the task is to cultivate a management practice that reaches for the divine in every society. This challenge is every bit as formidable as that encountered for the person above.

Christmas and the Church

"There are many things from which I might have derived good, by which I have not profited, I dare say," returned the nephew; "Christmas among the rest. But I am sure I have always thought of Christmas time, when it has come round—apart from the veneration due to its sacred name and origin, if anything belonging to it can be apart from that—as a good time; a kind of forgiving, charitable, pleasant time: the only time I know of, in the long calendar of the year, when men and women seem by one consent to open their shut-up hearts freely, and to think of people below them as if they really were fellow-passengers to the grave, and not another race of creatures bound on other journeys. And therefore, uncle, though it has never put a scrap of gold or silver in my pocket, I believe that it has *done me good and* will *do me good; and I say, God bless it!"*[240]

Large as the challenges to the good are in business education, and difficult as the tasks of fully honoring the person and society are in business practice, these challenges and tasks can be met, and I suppose must be met, in faith. There is direction and support to find in the world's religions and we would be wise, I believe, to turn to them for guidance.

With Scrooge's nephew above, I think of the power of Christmas and of the Catholic Church. In both I find direction and support for the good of business and of life generally. Of particular usefulness for business education, I suppose, are the doctrines of the Church to foster and protect the supreme good of the human person and society. Compiled in the Church's *Compendium of the Social Doctrine of the Church*, these doctrines include:

1) *Meaning and Unity*—the doctrines "must be appreciated in their unity, interrelatedness, and articulation";[241]

2) *The Principal of the Common Good*—"A society that wishes and intends to remain at the service of the human being at every level is a society that has the common good—the good of all people and of the whole person—as its primary goal";[242]

3) *The Universal Destination of Goods*—"Each person must have access to the level of well-being necessary for his full development";[243]

4) *The Principle of Subsidiarity*—"Every social activity ought of its very nature to furnish help to the members of the body social, and never destroy and absorb them";[244]

5) *Participation*—Provisions must be made for "activities by means of which the citizen, either as an individual or in association with others, whether directly or through representation, contributes to the cultural, economic, political, and social life of the civil community to which he belongs";[245]

6) *The Principle of Solidarity*—There must be recognition of "the intrinsic social nature of the human person, the equality of all in dignity and rights, and the common path of individuals and peoples toward an ever more committed unity";[246]

7) *The Fundamental Values of Social Life*—"All social values are inherent in the dignity of the human person, whose authentic development they foster. Essentially, these values are: truth, freedom, justice, love";[247]

8) *The Way of Love*—Love must be considered in its authentic value as the "highest and universal criterion of the whole of social ethics. Among all paths, even those sought and taken in order to respond to the ever new forms of current social questions, the 'more excellent way' is that marked out by love".[248]

In the secular university that has lost its human relation to God, I suppose that education in the good would do well to begin with such doctrines, or with like-minded statements of religious wisdom. I suppose that it is only in faith in God that we can find the beginning and end of the good, its *alpha* and *omega*. I suppose that this is the key to a business education and indeed the key to any education worthy of the name.

> *Scrooge was better than his word. He did it all, and infinitely more; and to Tiny Tim, who did NOT die, he was a second father. He became as good a friend, as good a master, and as good a man, as the good old city knew, or any other good old city, town, or borough, in the good old world. Some people laughed to see the alteration in him, but he let them laugh, and little heeded them; for he was wise enough to know that nothing ever happened on this globe for good at which some people did not have their fill of laughter at the outset; and know that such as these would be blind anyway, he thought it quite as well that they should wrinkle up their eyes in grins as have the malady in less attractive forms. His own heart laughed: and that was quite enough for him.*[249]

Chapter 7

The Joy of Business

We want for wonder, for a feeling of the great. Ours is an age of power-point pragmatism, without poetry and spirit. To purchase the great, we pay top dollar for "wonder-full" experiences—a grand vista, an erotic encounter, an exotic idyll, a roller coaster ride, a Hollywood fantasy—that in being "for sale" only confirm our poverty.

I am a student of this age—a student of business administration in particular, the most popular subject by far in the university today. Mine is the field that has turned the wonder of the human person into "human capital," a factor of production. And mine is the field that has defined a practice of management that defies all beauty and conscience. But at last, this chapter is not about the shortcomings of my field—which are familiar and of little moment—but about the wonder and joy my field cannot deny. It is a chapter to say that if we are going to do business without wonder and joy, then at least we should know what we are missing.

My argument is the plain one that joy in business is to find where all joy is to find; in the God who created and calls to us. With Saint Augustine we know that "Our hearts are restless until they rest in you dear Lord." But however plain this argument it challenges the many in business today, including the author, who do not always or even usually act as if God is the be all and end all. I want to show in this final chapter that, whether we know it or not and whether we want it or not, we come to joy in business as we come to God. This is the lesson of Faith, that God triumphs over mammon.

The Attitude of Wonder

"Wonder" is our word for the fact that behind the appearances of things that we know and say (what philosopher Immanuel Kant called 'phenomena') there is a truth we cannot know and say (what Kant called 'noumena'). This is the transcendental truth of God who creates all things in love and goodness.[250] His consciousness brings all things into being and life. Even lowly matter subsists in His spirit. Matter, according to poet Coleridge, is "that of which there is consciousness, but which is not itself conscious."[251] Although creative consciousness belongs to God, who creates all things, it belongs also to we who are created by God in His image. By our consciousness, which is God's gift to us, we share in His power to know and fashion creation. For writer Walker Percy wonder lies in the language by which we name and thereby bring into being all the fish of the sea, the birds of the air, and all the creatures that creepeth on the earth.[252] For psychologist Owen Barfield wonder lies in imagination whereby we discern (or better, 'divine') matter in spirit. For Barfield there is a "wonder-filled" gap between spirit and matter of which we must never lose sight. We must, he admonishes, never confuse our perceptions and abstractions for the truth of the world and never forget that what we call 'matter' is ever an appearance of spirit.[253] To the contrary, we must "save the appearances."[254] And for Barfield's friend and conspirator of the "Socratic Club" at Oxford, C.S. Lewis:

> The objects around me and my idea of 'me' will deceive if taken at their face value. But they are momentous if taken as the end-products of divine activities. Thus and not otherwise, the creation of matter and the creation of mind meet one another and the circuit is closed...[255]

Thus, in wonder, faith unites spirit and matter, mind and body, and thereby keeps whole what Descartes and enlightenment science tore asunder (to our unending confusion today). Faith warns of the dangers of conforming too closely to the "truths" of science which are only about matter and not about spirit. For all it teaches about nature, science teaches little about the scientist himself, who is not of nature but of God. When it comes to a study of man—to anthropology—faith is greater than science because it bears truths science cannot reach.[256] C.S. Lewis compared the two saying that if science were the notes to a poem, faith would be the poem itself. And likewise G.K. Chesterton saw in faith a science illumined by romance. Faith is "the great tale that is true."[257] Only in the wonder of faith do we come to the mystery of human being.

Wonder is to know in the miracles of creation; miracles that even the most hard-bitten atheist cannot deny. Cosmologists can give no reason for the cosmos; geologists, no reason for the firm and agreeable earth of warm seas and blanket of atmosphere; biologists, no reason for the life that teems throughout; and philosophers, no reason for reason itself. And in what must be the miracle of miracles, all of it—the cosmos, earth, life, and mind—is precisely geared for our human being. It seems that "in the Creator's plan, created realities, which are good in themselves, exist for man's use."[258] The wonder of wonders is that man is made in the image and likeness of God and for that knows what no other creature on earth can know; namely, that God's illimitable love is the supreme miracle of being.

Joy to the World

Where there is creation there is the wonder and joy of God who is love. In Jesus Christ we know that God's joy comes particularly in His creation of man in His image. And by the same token, in Jesus Christ we know that our joy comes in fulfilling His will as we, together with others, extend His creation in the world. To create is to take part in Gods love through Christ.

Work is a Wonder and Joy

As we have seen, among the wonders and ways to joy is work. According to John Paul II: "Man works because he is like God." "Among all the creatures of the world," he continues, "only man works consciously. The animals are very active, but none works in the sense of human work."[259] Seen rightly, in its full humanness, work is the means by which man takes part in God's creation. It is "an expression of man's full humanity, in his historical and his eschatological orientation. Man's free and responsible action reveals his intimate relationship with the Creator and his creative power."[260] He is God's agent on earth. "By his work and industriousness, man—who has a share in the divine art and wisdom—makes creation, the cosmos already ordered by the Father, more beautiful. He summons the social and community energies that increase the common good."[261] The joy of work thus is the joy of creation. What is more, the joy of work is the joy of salvation. "Human work is presented to us as redeemed...the Gospel of work proclaims that every person who works in union with Christ shares in the Redemption which he accomplished. Work thus takes on a new value for man: it becomes something sacred."[262] Work is an everyday wonder and joy oriented to eternal wonder and joy.

Moments of Creation in Business

The wonder and joy of business appear in its essential movements or "moments" of creation: namely, love, play, and individuation. *Love* is the first moment and root of creation; the dynamism of a human life that is always and everywhere a division in unity. Love is the form and feeling that abides in the tension between the unity of human being and its myriad divisions of person, family, group, team, business, community, culture, nation, race, and religion. In the same way that love is revealed in the coming together of divided persons (e.g., in the nuptial union of male and female in one flesh), love in business is revealed in the coming together of divided persons, groups, teams, and departments within the firm, and in the coming together of competitors within the marketplace. As any entrepreneur can attest, love is the very stuff of business. The internal key to business success is cooperative conflict among business processes and functions—what business scholar Mary Parker Follett called "integrative unity."[263] The external key to business success is to find and fulfill a place or "niche" in the economy that serves the needs of others. To be in such a place in the vital unity of the economy is to be, literally, in love.

Play is the second moment and leading edge of creation; it is the advancing wave of love in a human life that is always changing its form. Through play old loves—that is, old divisions in unity—are overturned (in a process economist Joseph Schumpeter called "creative destruction") and new loves are formed to take their place. This is the creative dynamic in which young girls playing dolls imagine new forms of social relation and in which young boys (and older boys too) playing sports create new hierarchies of winners and losers. And this is the creative dynamic of business in which product designers, advertisers, and even public relations officials imagine new social realities and in which executives, salespeople, and financiers compete for standing in the market. Business is an arena of creative play as sure as any in childhood, only a little more grown up and perhaps a little less friendly.

At last there is *individuation,* the third moment and glory of human creation; the culmination of love as it is transformed by play. Individuation is the moment of identity in which a person or group comes into being as a distinctive person in the whole of a community. It is the uniquely human condition of being at once a unique person whole unto oneself *and* a fully integrated member of a larger community. For a newborn child individuation appears in the miracle of a new personality in the family (usually a surprise to everyone, except perhaps to mother who may have sensed what was coming). For a new business individuation appears in the magical coming together of the elements of viability (of capital, innovation, market, and management). And for an established business individuation appears in the constant morphing of act and purpose that keeps the enterprise fresh and new. Thus we see that what begins in love becomes through play an ever unique identity, an individuation. A new person or business comes into being; an older person and established business is renewed. This story of love transformed by play to create new life is the story of human life in God; it is the story of wonder and joy to find as much in business as anywhere else.

A Case in Point: The AES Corporation

The wonder and joy of business are more than just hopeful ideas; they are realities to discover in business practice. Such realities are well-developed and ably-chronicled in the practices of the AES Corporation, an "energy solutions" company that provides electrical power to people and businesses across the globe. As told by its co-founder and CEO, Dennis Bakke, in a book entitled *Joy at Work*, AES was dedicated to creating a joyful workplace. "My hypothesis," he wrote, "was that a fun workplace is one that allows people to work in an environment that is most consistent with human nature."[264]

Although Bakke did not put it in quite these terms, the story of AES is that of helping employees realize the joy of creation by achieving *individuation* through *play* founded on *love*. Individuation was the goal. According to Bakke, the first priority of the business, before even profit or any other metric of business success, was to create a joyful workplace that "gives all workers an opportunity to make important decisions and take significant actions using their gifts and skills to the utmost."[265] By design, if not always in effect, workers were given as much opportunity as possible to realize their personal being, their vocation, through their contributions to the community as a whole. And play was the means to this joyful individuation. As described by Bakke, this was achieved in several ways, but particularly by two innovations in company management: first, a so-called "honeycomb" structure that joined employees in small multi-skilled self-managed work teams, each responsible for its own area of the business; and second, the "advice process" whereby even low-level employees were given authority to make consequential business decisions in their area, provided that in doing so they seek the advice of those around them. Together these management innovations fostered individuation by "answering the age-old organizational dilemma of how to embrace the rights and needs of the individual while simultaneously ensuring the successful functioning of the team, community, or company."[266] The result was an organization comprised of what Bakke called "banana split" teams:

> The kind of teams I am suggesting are more like banana splits than milkshakes. Milkshakes blend the various flavors of ice cream, toppings milk, and other ingredients into one undifferentiated dessert. In banana splits, each scoop of vanilla, chocolate, and strawberry ice cream, along with the bananas and toppings, remain separate until eaten. In a banana split team, individuals play special roles and maintain their identities. The sum of the parts is greater than the whole.[267]

With the honeycomb structure and advice process in place, AES could satisfy what Bakke calls "the primary factor in determining whether people experience joy or drudgery in the workplace;" namely, the "degree to which they control their work."[268] Last, but not least, all of this was made possible by love—the first moment of creation—and in particular by that love that sees and supports the dignity of each and every person at work. This is the lesson of most if not all faith traditions, certainly the lesson of Christ, and the lesson that Bakke sees more clearly than most business leaders:

> "Love" is not a word used much in the rough-and-tumble corporate world, perhaps because it sounds soft and sentimental. But as Max De Pree says, ... "We are working primarily for love." ... Leaders who create dynamic, rewarding, enjoyable workplaces love people. Love is an act of humility that says, "I need you." Love affirms that the other person is worthy and important. Most of us know what love demands.[269]

Truths Known All Along

Although the joy of God in business may seem farfetched to the secular ears of today's business intelligentsia, we have always had the idea of it, albeit in terms that do not give God His due. Bringing the theology of business to the fore highlights truths written plainly and indelibly on the heart. Chief among these is that He is our heart's desire and joy.

The joy of God lies behind what scientists tell us about work. Theories about work psychology—theories of job design which delineate characteristics of jobs that satisfy and motivate;[270] theories of work impact which trace how the good of jobs warms the hearts of their holders;[271] theories about work motivation which catalogue the needs evoked and met on the job;[272] and theories of heroism which detail the need for meaning at work[273]—take new color and greater depth in the light of God. Work that is satisfying, impactful, rewarding, and meaningful is work that calls to spiritual being in the will and way of God. It is joyful work that allows us to take our unique part in God's creation and that allows us to give ourselves to others in the love of God. This is what is ultimately satisfying, impactful, rewarding, and meaningful about it. To speak only scientifically about work is to leave out the source and final explanation of our joy. While scientists may be averse to God's "intrusion" in the clock-workings of the natural world, we speak on God's behalf when our hearts cry out for those who do not have work or for whom work alienates them from themselves and from others. In such feelings, which we can hardly deny, we give voice to the Divine.

A sounding of divinity was to hear recently from John Bogle, investment pioneer and founder of the Vanguard Mutual Funds Group, in a rueful commencement speech to MBA graduates at Georgetown University. His subject was money management. His title was "Enough."

> *Enough.* I was stunned by its simple eloquence, to say nothing of its relevance to some of the vital issues arising in American society today. Many of them revolve around money—yes, *money*—increasingly, in our "bottom line" society, the Great God of prestige, the Great Measure of the Man (and Woman). So this morning I have the temerity to ask you soon-to-be-minted MBA graduates, most of whom will enter the world of commerce, to consider with me the role of "enough" in business and entrepreneurship in our society, "enough" in the dominant role of the financial system in our economy, and "enough" in the values you will bring to the fields you choose for your careers. …
>
> We're moving, or so it seems, to a world where we're no longer *making* anything in this country; we're merely *trading* pieces of paper, swapping stocks and bonds back and forth with one another, and paying our financial croupiers a veritable fortune…. Once a profession in which business was subservient, the field of money management and Wall Street has become a business in which the profession is subservient. Harvard Business School Professor Rakesh Khurana was right when he defined the conduct of a true professional with these words: "*I will create value for society, rather than extract it.*" And yet money management, by definition, extracts value from the returns earned by

our business enterprises. Warren Buffett's wise partner Charlie Munger lays it on the line:

> Most money-making activity contains profoundly antisocial effects... As high-cost modalities become ever more popular ... the activity exacerbates the current harmful trend in which ever more of the nation's ethical young brain-power is attracted into lucrative money-management and its attendant modern fictions, as distinguished from work providing much more value to others.[274]

Bogle wants his MBA charges to put their profession of money making into the larger context of what is good for themselves and others. The good that is too much ignored in money management today is just that of creation, of making things of value for others. That is the good of work that connects us to the creative will of God.

There is the joy of God as well in what scientists tell us about business. Economic theories of the firm—models of shareholder value, stakeholder claims, and the nexus of contracts—take new color and depth in the light of God. Then it is clear that business begins in creative spirit—at the outset in that of the individual entrepreneur but later in that of the entire organization—in meeting the needs of others.[275] Then it is clear that the corporation is not only or mainly for its shareholders, for its stakeholders, or even for its nexus of contracts, but rather that for the creative imperative that joins man in the will of God. Economic models of the firm are glosses on this truth, representations that capture some but not all of man's economic initiative, or what might be called his business impulse. According to John Czarnetzky:

> The corporation arises for a very specific reason, one that also goes to the heart of the Catholic understanding of work itself: corporations are formed and grow to provide a suitable locus for entrepreneurship, a special kind of work consisting of the exercise of economic judgment which reveals, in the words of the Church, the full humanity of individuals as "creative and relational subjects."[276]

Thus the wonder and joy of business reaches to the core of our being. It is the truth we have known all along; the truth written on our hearts that we know even as we pretend to Godless scientific objectivity. The joy of God abides.

Business and the Church

In its deepest humanity, business is liturgical—a realization of our true human being, our person in community with others in God. In this liturgical aspect business is an emblem and arm of the Church. As Church teaching reminds us:

> Economic activity and material progress must be placed at the service of man and society. If people dedicate themselves to these with the faith, hope and love of Christ's disciples, even the economy and progress can be transformed into places of salvation and sanctification. In these areas too it is possible to express a love and a solidarity that are more than human, and to contribute to the growth of a new humanity that anticipates the world to come. Jesus sums up all of revelation in calling the believer to become rich before God (cf. LK 12:21). The economy too is useful to this end, when its function as an instrument for the overall growth of man and society, of the human quality of life, is not betrayed. [277]

Viewed at this highest reach, in this sacramental way, business becomes beautiful. Its beauty, as Romano Guardini describes, "is the triumphant splendor which breaks forth when the hidden truth is revealed, when the external phenomenon is at all points the perfect expression of inner essence."[278] At this moment we know why the center of business holds; because its center is God.

To the question: "How can business make straight our path to God?" comes the answer: "By taking part in the Church" which is our true guide to joy—put here on earth by God for that purpose. The teachings of the Church lead to joy by leading to God. And the sacraments of the Church nourish the way by drawing upon the strength of Christ. The Church calls us to joy in the liturgy of the Mass which is the image par excellence of our being in God. The Mass is the universal image of the Church, of all human persons everywhere, both living and dead, united in communion with Christ. The Mass is the image of love; of divided persons each a unique and infinitely valued child of God, joined together with all mankind in worship of God. The Mass thus is a model and guide to the spiritual possibilities of business—it is an especially refined instance of people directing their efforts together to God. Business becomes a liturgy as it likewise conveys the feeling and form of human being in God.

The distinction often and casually drawn between Church and business (or between Church and the state) is substantially false and certainly misleading. Although given to different ends—the one to eternal ends, the other to temporal ends—these ends are not disjoined and opposed but are ordered to one another. In particular, the secular ends of business are subordinate to and serve the sacred ends of the Church. Human life is essentially and supremely spiritual and all that man does is properly ordered to this end. Thus instead of being contraries, as usually imagined, the Church and business are points on a continuum measured by degrees of spiritual fulfillment or realization. Where the Church may anchor the scale with the richest and most compelling image of man's spiritual being, all human institutions, including those of business, are engaged with this image and approximate it to one degree or another. The danger comes when these so-called "secular" institutions invoke their own prophets and gods; when they suppose that their worldly material ends supersede the eternal ends of the Church; when they in effect become their own church apart from God. Then these institutions work against man's being; against the wonder and joy of his life in God. When this happens in business we see but a facsimile of human being. In place of the real spiritual person (who is literally 'of son' to God) we have the ersatz 'person' of the economic individual. In place of the real love of community in God, we have the ersatz 'love' of corporate culture. It is to the Church that business must turn to awaken and nourish the spirit of those it exists to serve. If business is to be for man as the Church is for man, it must take its place in cooperation with the Church in helping man reach for God.

Thus although business can and should be distinguished from the Church, its fate is tied to the Church. Business serves the good of man only as it recognizes and supports the Church's right to exist and propagate the faith. As theologian Antonio Rosmini notes, because the Church comprises the universal society of human being in God, it is the supreme good to which all other human societies, including those of business, must bow:

> Moreover, because this society [the society of the Church] is the highest and only true good, it is supreme amongst the societies of the faithful, all of which must refer to it, and serve it. Just as lesser goods are not good unless referred to the supreme good, so societies are not upright but only sects and conspiracies unless they serve the supreme society, which alone renders other societies morally possible and just.[279]

In conclusion, while these pages have not tried to present programs or panaceas for business, it is hoped that they go some way to free the mind to think about business in a more fruitful way—in particular, to see that business abides in God; to see that work is to create a world in God's image according to His will; and to see that when these conditions are met there is love in God. This is the wonder and joy of business to seek here and now as prelude to the greatest wonder and joy of all to seek ever after.

Notes

1. John Paul II, In Gary Atkinson, Robert G. Kennedy & Michael Naughton (eds.), *Dignity of Work: John Paul II Speaks to Managers and Workers* (Lanham, MD: University Press of America, 1995), p. 64

2. Lloyd E. Sandelands, *An Anthropological Defense of God* (New Brunswick, NJ: Transaction, 2007)

3. John Paul II, *Dignity of Work*, 59

4. Ibid, 53

5. Ibid, 77

6. William James, *The Varieties of Religious Experience* (London: Longmans, Greene & Company, 1902), p. 139.

7. John Paul II, Laborem Exercens, 1981: http://www.vatican.va/edocs/ENG0217/INDEX.HTM

8. Fredrick Taylor, *The Principles of Scientific Management* (New York: Norton, 1911)

9. Ibid, p. 29

10. About this, Taylor (1911) was certain and relentless:

> The writer asserts as a general principle ... that in almost all of the mechanic arts the science which underlies each act of each workman is so great and amounts to so much that the workman who is best suited to actually doing the work is incapable of fully understanding this science, without the guidance and help of those who are working with him or over him, either through lack of education or through insufficient mental capacity. In order that the work may be done in accordance with scientific laws, it is necessary that there shall be a far more equal division of the responsibility between the management and the workmen than exists under any of the ordinary types of management (p. 26).

11. Edward Jones, *The Administration of Industrial Enterprises* (New York: Longmans, Greene, & Company, 1918), pp. 147-148. It wasn't long, however, before even the "artful" elements of handling men were claimed by scientific management. According to L. Urwick "Scientific management was an affirmation that the methods of thought, the respect for natural law, which inspired the work of chemists and engineers, could and should be applied to the human arrangements underlying the use of the new and powerful tools they had evolved"—see L. Urwick, *The Elements of Administration* (New York: Harper Brothers, 1943).

12. Elton Mayo, *Problems of Industrial Civilization* (Boston: Harvard University, 1945).

13. Chris Argyris, *Personality and Organization* (New York: Harper & Row, 1957).

14. Douglas McGregor, *The Human Side of Enterprise* (New York: McGraw-Hill, 1960). McGregor's Theory X illustrates the self-fulfilling aspect of scientific management. Theory X describes how workers act when managers treat them as factors of production, conceive them as motions to control in time and space, and divide them in body and mind.

15. Thomas Peters & Robert Waterman, *In Search of Excellence* (New York: Warner Books, 1982)

16. Gerald F. Davis, *Managed by the Market* (New York: Oxford University Press, 2009)

17. Peters & Waterman, p. xxi

18. Ibid, p. xxii

19. Ernest Becker, *The Birth and Death of Meaning* (New York: Free Press, 1971)

20. See Barbara Ehrenreich, *Bait and Switch* (New York: Owl Books, 2006)

21. Michael Kinsley, "We try harder (but what's the point?)" *New York Times*, 05.16.07

22. See Lloyd Sandelands, *An Anthropological Defense of God* (New Brunswick, NJ: Transaction, 2007)

23. Milton Friedman & Rose Friedman, *Free to Choose* (New York: Harcourt, Brace & Jovanovich, 1980), p. 21.

24. John Paul II, *Centesimus Annus*, http://www.vatican.va/edocs/ENG0214/INDEX.HTM, #42

25. Ibid, #43

26. Owen Barfield, *Saving the Appearances* (Middleton, CT: Wesleyan, 1965)

27. Leon Kass, *Life, Liberty, and the Defense of Dignity* (San Francisco: Encounter Books, 2002)

28. Soren Kierkegaard, quoted in Karl Stern, *The Flight from Woman* (New York: Farrar, Straus & Giroux, 1965, p. 56-57.

29. Michael Novak, *Business as a Calling* (New York: Free Press, 1996)

30. Romano Guardini, *The Spirit of the Liturgy* (New York: Herder & Herder, 1998), p. 62.

31. See Robert Heilbronner, *The Worldly Philosophers* (New York: Time, Inc., 1961)

32. Today such thinking is showcased in schools of business administration which raise economic theory to the status of a religion and which present business as being almost entirely a problem of maximizing value for shareholders. Having lost its feel for the human, business education cedes inner being to outer circumstances. Perhaps this is why more than a few business students today feel that their education lacks soul.

33. Indeed, this is the catastrophe well and presciently described by Christian apologist and literary scholar C.S. Lewis (2001) as the 'abolition of man':

> We reduce things to mere Nature in order that we may 'conquer' them. We are always conquering Nature, because 'Nature' is the name for what we have, to some extent, conquered. The price of conquest is to treat a thing as mere Nature. ... As long as this process stops short of the final stage we may well hold that the gain outweighs the loss. But as soon as we take the final step of reducing our own species to the level of mere Nature, the whole process is stultified, for this time the being who stood to gain and the being who has been sacrificed are one and the same. (p. 71)

34. Max Weber, *The Protestant Ethic and the Spirit of Capitalism* (New York: Scribner's Sons, 1958)

35. Robert Jackall, *Moral Mazes* (New York: Oxford University Press, 1988)

36. Marya Mannes, *But will it sell?* (Philadelphia: Lippincott, 1964), p. 17

37. Benjamin Barber, *Consumed* (New York: Norton, 2007)

38. Thomas Frank, *One Market Under God* (New York: Vintage, 2002)

39. Ibid, p. 219

40. William James, *Pragmatism and Other Essays* (New York: Washington Square Books, 1963), p. 23

41. Ibid, p. 26

42. Walker Percy, *Lost in the Cosmos* (New York: Picador, 1983)

43. The cataclysm of naming is illuminated by the story of Helen Keller. Denied the vision and hearing that might have connected her to others, Helen spent her early childhood as an isolated and "difficult" child. Despite this she was taught by her loving teacher, Miss Sullivan, a number of hand signs by which she could indicate her desires for food and water and such. To this point Miss Sullivan communicated with her as we might with a dog, not by ideas or concepts, but by signs of things. But then came the magical day and moment when her life was changed—completely, irrevocably, and joyfully. Helen signaled to Miss Sullivan that she wanted a drink of water. Bringing her to the fountain, Miss Sullivan put one of Helen's hands under the running water while making the sign for water in the other hand. In that moment, for reasons that remain a mystery, Helen made the discovery of a lifetime; namely, that the finger tapping in her one hand was not only a sign of the water in her other hand, but much, much more than that; it was a name for water itself. In that moment, Helen came to her first idea, her first draught of meaning. She spent the rest of that day and, indeed, every day after, eagerly and joyfully learning the names everything around her. At last her isolation ended, she joined the human world of meaning. In that moment—it seems shocking and even hyperbolic to say—Helen herself came into being.

44. Percy, *Lost in the Cosmos*

45. Blaise Pascal, *Thoughts* (selections) (London: J.M. Dent, 1931), p. 24, #171

46. David Bakke, *Joy at Work* (Seattle, WA: PVG)

47. John Budziszewski, *What We Can't Not Know* (Dallas: Spence, 2004)

48. See John Paul II, *Laborem Exercens*

49. This is a point made effectively by Ernest Becker, who began his book, *The Birth and Death of Meaning* (New York: Free Press, 1971) upon a dare. Repeat to your self, he enjoined, the sentence "man is an animal." It cannot be done long or easily, for there is more to man than his animal nature. Man is not only, or even mainly, a creature; he is a being, human being. Man is the one being in creation that seeks and makes meaning

50. See Walker Percy, *Lost in the Cosmos* (New York: Picador, 1983). This chapter takes some of its content and much of its inspiration from Percy, who showed how man is a mystery to himself and how he gets into trouble in trying to make his life meaningful.

51. How ironic it is that even the greatest students of man, such as Charles Darwin and Sigmund Freud, could not by their science account for themselves. As Walker Percy has remarked, Darwin writing in his study in Kent could explain the appearance of all forms of life on earth except for that of himself writing about the appearance of all forms of life on earth; see *Signposts in a Strange Land* (New York: Picador, 1991).

52. See Lloyd Sandelands, *An Anthropological Defense of God* (New Brunswick, NJ: Transaction, 2007).

53. John Paul II, *Fides et Ratio* (Vatican. 1998, p. 5).

54. John Paul II, *Crossing the Threshold of Hope* (London: Alfred A. Knopf, 1994)

55. Cardinal Josef Ratzinger, *Introduction to Christianity* (San Francisco: Ignatius Press, 1990), p. 452

56. Martin Buber, *I and Thou* (New York: Charles Scribner's Sons, 1958)

57. Pope Benedict XVI, *Vatican Information Service*, 02.21.07

58. Rosamund S Zander and Benjamin Zander, *The Art of Possibility*, (New York: Penguin, 2002) contrast the "world of measurement" at work, in which we die to human being, with the "world of possibility" at work, in which we come to life with others. Their distinction parallels that of this chapter between "work against being" and "work

for being"; the main difference is that where the Zanders are vague about the meaning of possibility, I identify it with ultimate being in God.

59. This sin of misappropriation is known to philosophy as the "fallacy of misplaced concreteness" (see A.N. Whitehead, *Science and the Modern World*, (New York: Macmillan, 1925)) and/or as the "failure to save the appearances" (see Owen Barfield, *Saving the Appearances*, (Middletown, CT: Wesleyan, 1965)). These are phrases for the excess of naturalism in which objects named are mistaken as real (as existing apart from the subject who does the naming). The excess of naturalism is met by the excess of humanism in which objects named are mistaken as imaginary (as not existing apart from the subject who does the naming). An example of the peril in these two ways of thinking about the world is the way sexuality is regarded these days, at one extreme as an objective animal function and at the other extreme as mere whim – see Lloyd Sandelands, *Man and Nature in God* (New Brunswick, NJ: Transaction, 2005).

60. Pope Benedict, *VIS*, 02.21.07

61. Kahlil Gibran, *The Prophet* (New York: Alfred Knopf, 1923), p. 26.

62. *Catechism of the Catholic Church* (Article 2427; p. 642-3)

63. *Ibid*, Article 2428, p. 643

64. Leo Tolstoy, *A calendar of wisdom: Daily thoughts to nourish the soul, written and selected from the world's sacred texts*, translated by P. Sekirin. (New York: Scribner, 1997), p. 152.

65. Bailie, G. 2004. The subject of *Gaudium et Spes*: Reclaiming a Christocentric anthropology of the human person, p. 23. www.stthomas.edu/cathstudies/CST /conferences/gaudium/papers/Bailie.pdf

66. As the Catholic Church notes: "the more that human realities are seen in the light of God's plan and lived in communion with God, the more they are empowered and liberated in their distinctive identity and in the freedom that is proper to them" (*Compendium of the Social Doctrine of the Church*, 2004, p. 20, #45).

67. This concrete idea of love is captured by Carter Heyward: "Love is not fundamentally a sweet feeling; not, at heart, a matter of sentiment, attachment, or being "drawn toward." Love is active, effective, a matter of making reciprocal and mutually beneficial relation with one's friends and enemies." http://thinkexist.com/quotes/with/keyword/make_love/3.html

68. Although the three vocations can be distinguished in concept, they are images of one another in experience. Love is a kind of play in which we individuate to become a person. These vocations unite in God as aspects of His being. These vocations are the soil of human being from which flower the many varied forms of social life, including language, culture, art, science, technology, and, not least, work.

69. Moreover, this may be necessary if the work is to be any good. This point is made Walker Percy who found the good in his work only with the loss of all external concerns. Good work is possible, he wrote, only after one has given up on himself and his prospects; only after one is washed-up alone on the beach, shipwrecked, with nothing but an honest will to live. See Percy, *Signposts in a Strange Land*, 1991.

70. See Lloyd Sandelands, *Thinking about Social Life* (Lanham, MD: University Press of America), 33-51.

71. Mark Twain, http://www.onthepage.org/work/quotes.htm

72. Henry C. Metcalf & L Urwick, Eds., *Dynamic Administration: The Collected Papers of Mary Parker Follett* (New York: Harper & Brothers, 1942), p. 268.

73. *Ibid*, p. 209

74. D. Stephen Long, "Corporations and the common good," *Ave Marie Law Review*, Winter 2006, p. 87

75. David Millon, "Theories of the corporation," *Duke Law Journal*, 1990, No. 2, pp. 201-262

76. R.H. Coase, "The nature of the firm," *Economica, 4(16),* 1937: 386-405, p. 393

77. James G. March & Herbert H. Simon, *Organizations* (New York: John Wiley, 1958)

78. Emile Durkheim, *The Division of Labor in Society*, translated by G. Simpson, (New York: Macmillan, 1933); Kenneth Arrow, "Methodological individualism and social knowledge," *American Economic Association Papers and Proceedings*, May 1-9, 1994

79. Helen J. Alford & Michael J. Naughton, *Managing as if Faith Mattered: Christian Principles in the Modern Organization* (Notre Dame, IN: Notre Dame University Press, 2001).

80. M.P. Follett, *Dynamics of Administration*, p. 200.

81. See W. Richard Scott & Gerald F. Davis, *Organizations and Organizing: Rational, Natural, and Open-systems Perspectives* (New York: Prentice-Hall, 2007).

82. http://dictionary.oed.com

83. M.P. Follett, *Dynamics of Administration*, p. 268.

84. Ibid, p. 294

85. Ibid, p. 218

86. *Genesis* 1.27

87. This Old Testament idea of union in God is enriched by the New Testament idea of the Trinity. As God is a unity of divided persons—of Father, Son, and Holy Spirit—we are an image of God in a unity of divided persons—of male and female.

88. *Catechism of Catholic Church* (New York: Doubleday, 1995), p. 590.

89. For a more extensive description of how the forms of human society originate in and are sustained by the functional relating of male and female, see my *Male and Female in Social Life* (New Brunswick, NJ: Transaction, 2001). In that book, however, I had not yet come to see that this relating depends for its integrity upon a unifying third term. In a word, I had not yet come to see that this relating rests in God.

90. The discussion in this section borrows from my *Man and Nature in God* (New Brunswick, NJ: Transaction, 2005), pp. 32-40.

91. The precursors of family appear in the primary order of mammalian and primate social life described earlier. Among our mammal ancestors the hubbub of hierarchy-obsessed males clamoring to impress choosy females produced only brief impersonal assignations—flings with no strings. Females mated the highest-ranking males (in some species the alpha male almost exclusively) and, once pregnant, left the sexual stage to care for the young in the female group. Later, females of certain primate species (including the precursors of modern baboons, chimpanzees, and humans), granted sexual favors also to males who consistently helped them with food and children—males that could be described as 'friends;' see Barbara Smuts, *Sex and Friendship in Baboons* (New York: Aldine de Gruyter, 1985). And so was inaugurated a sexual economy in which males were sexually rewarded not only for being dominant, but also for being reliably helpful. This development was crucial because it meant that a great many more males could gain access to females. In principle, if not in fact, every male could befriend a female and thereby gain mating chances that otherwise belonged to the dominant male.

92. So congenial is family to human existence that we might wonder if it was a consequence of hominid migration onto the savannah or a factor contributing to this migration. With family to stabilize relations between the sexes, hominid females could cooperate in mutual support with minimal concern for who among them would capture the attention and resources of which males, while hominid males could cooperate for mutual gain in group tasks with likewise minimal concern about which of them would mate which females. Family facilitates cooperation within and between sexes; see H.E. Fisher, *The Sex Contract: Evolution of Human Behavior* (New York: William Morrow, 1982).

93. The psychology of this functional unity is perhaps familiar. In the most robust men's or women's groups there is a hint of family, and likewise in the warmest and coziest domestic scene there is a brooding presence of single sex groups. One enters a men's or women's group in part to leave family behind and in part to prepare for a return. Men learn to compete fairly with other men so as to be attractive to women. Women learn to make wise choices and to care for young so as to be attractive to men. By the same token, one seeks a family life in part to leave the men's or women's group behind and in part to set the stage for a return. In the family, men and women learn how the other feels, thinks, and acts. However, while love of mate and love of children make man and woman whole, this comes at the risk of losing one's sexual identity, which must be reclaimed in the same sex group.

94. Susanne Langer, *Mind: An Essay on Human Feeling, Vol. 1* (Baltimore, MD: Johns Hopkins, 1967)

95. This awareness is unprecedented in animal life and changes everything about human social life. Where other animals *have* parts in species life (think of castes of social insects or sexual divisions of labor in mammals), people *play* parts in species life. Where a worker bee never worries its destiny and never thinks to throw off the chains that bind it to the hive, people worry all the time about who they are and about their duties to others. A man is no pigeon in a pecking order, he is a self- and socially-aware member of a group. Hierarchy for him is both a bodily fact and a cultural idea. Places in the hierarchy are "roles" played by more or less interchangeable group members.

96. Karl Stern, *The Flight from Woman* (New York: Farrar, Straus & Giroux, 1965), p. xx. See also my *Male and Female in Social Life* (New Brunswick, NJ: Transaction, 2001).

97. Margaret Mead, *Male and female* (New York: Morrow, 1949).

98. From the ages-old and heavenly wisdom of Genesis we come to the late and hellish distortions of Sigmund Freud and others who likewise put sex at the center of human life but in an inhuman way. Sex is significant, not for its polymorphous perversity, but for its realization of the divine. The human heart longs for God and takes joy in moments of divine communion.

99. These several ideas about incorporation are consolidated in the social teaching of the Catholic Church under the 'principle of subsidiarity.' According to this principle the full and total aim of all human society, including those of business, is to image God, which it must do in two ways: 1) by honoring the dignity of the human person (who is made in the image of God); and 2) by honoring the human family (which in union of male and female is also the image of God). This honoring of person and family must take place at every level of human life.

100. *Matthew* 22:36

101. D. Stephen Long, "Corporations and the common good," op cit.

102. David Millon, "Theories of the corporation," op. cit.

103. We compensate for the deadening abstractions of such modern thinking by cheap sensation and empty pleasure—we fill our lives with exciting images, tellingly with images that are often sexual in nature. However, instead of answering the true call of our male and female being (the call to love by God), we seek to control sex for ourselves to make its power our own. It is a monumentally arrogant undertaking that is both hopeless and wrong. We fail to see that love is a sacramental image of our being in God. And we fail to see that power has divine roots in love, in the attraction and influence of male and female—that the overt power of male differentiation (reflected in assertions of one kind or another) is elicited, met and matched by the covert power of female unity (reflected in receptivity and nurture), and vice versa. In sin we do not see that we have lost our connection to the source and true meaning of incorporation; namely that we are male and female in God. As a result, our sexual energy and power, which cannot be denied, lose their moorings and needful limits and take grotesque forms in character neuroses of hyper-activism, icy rationalism, and narcissism as well as in sexual cruelties and harassments of various kinds.

104. As noted by theologian Joyce Little: "Scientific/technological man (Big Brother) and feminist woman (Big Sister) both operated on the same principle and for the same reason: both are in thrall to abstraction, abstraction from the limits of nature, from the limits of history, from the limits of human bodiliness." *The Church and the Culture War* (San Francisco: Ignatius Press, 1995), p. 62.

105. This is *not* an argument for or against equal opportunity in the workplace, but is instead an argument for living in truth. It her wisdom, the Church distinguishes the lives of men and women in society. Of men, Pope John Paul II writes in his apostolic exhortation *Familaris Consortio* (December 16, 1996): "Within the conjugal and family communion-community, the man is called upon to live his gift and role as husband and father" (p. 17). And of women, John Paul II writes: "While it must be recognized that women have the same right as men to perform various public functions, society must be structured in such a way that wives and mothers are 'not in practice compelled' to work outside the home, and that their families can live and prosper in a dignified way even when they themselves devoted their full time to their own family. Further-more, the mentality which honors women more for their work outside the home than for their work within the family must be overcome" (p. 16-17).

106. Pope Pius XI, 1931, Encyclical Letter, Rerum Novarum, www.vatican.va/; Pope John Paul II, 1981, Encyclical Letter, *Laborem Exercens*, www.vatican.va/; and Pope John Paul II, 1991, Encyclical Letter: *Centesimus Annus*, www.vatican.va/

107. Jean-Yves Calvez & Micahel. J. Naughton, "Catholic social teaching and the purpose of the business organization." In S.A. Cortright & M.J. Naughton (eds), *Rethinking the Purpose of Business*. (Notre Dame, IN: Notre Dame University, 2002), pp. 3-22.

108. D. Stephen Long, "Corporations and the common good," op cit.

109. Timothy L. Fort, "Business as a mediating institution." In S.A. Cortright & M.J. Naughton (eds), *Rethinking the Purpose of Business*. (Notre Dame, IN: Notre Dame University, 2002)

110. This is an idea that has for many years and in many ways been championed by Robert Greenleaf. See Anne T. Spears, Larry Greenleaf & Robert Fraker, *Seeker and Servant: Reflections on Religious Leadership* (San Francisco: Jossey-Bass, 1996)

111. Mary Follett, *Dynamics of Administration*, p. 269.

112. Romano Guardini, *The End of the Modern World* (Wilmington, DL: ISI Books, 1998), 119.

113. Mary Parker Follett, In *Dynamic Administration: The collected papers of Mary Parker Follett*, H.C. Metcalf & L. Urwick (eds.) (New York: Harper and Brothers, 1942), 294.

114. Cited in Jeffrey Pfeffer, *Managing with Power* (Boston, MA: Harvard Business School, 1992), p. 8

115. Ibid, 11

116. Ibid, 12

117. John R.P. French & Bertram Raven, "The bases of social power." In D. Cartwright (ed.), *Studies in Social Power* (Ann Arbor, MI: The University of Michigan).

118. Warren Bennis and Burt Nanus, *Leaders: The Strategies for Taking Charge* (New York: Harper and Row, 1985), 17.

119. Pfeffer, *Managing with Power*, 30

120. Robert B. Cialdini, "Harnessing the science of persuasion," *Harvard Business Review*, October, 2001, 74

121. Ibid, 340

122. Jeffrey Pfeffer, however, nearly does come out and say so. "The end," he writes, "may not always justify the means, but neither should it automatically be used to discredit the means." Ibid, 16

123. Alasdair MacIntyre, *After Virtue*, 2e (Notre Dame, IN: University of Notre Dame Press), 74

124. Romano Guardini, *The End of the Modern World* (Wilmington, DL: ISI Books, 1998), 128

125. As Guardini points out, in comparing the power of man to other animals: "At first glance it might seem that man is engaged in a similar process—that is, supplementing his bodily functions with certain objects which intensify those functions. In reality, right from the start, there is something in man which does not exist in the animal; man is aware—who can say how?—of the relation between cause and effect. He senses, even though he may not understand, the significance *behind* the forms and patterns of life, and he directs each aspect toward the realization of that meaning. In other words, his spirit is at work. Man rises above his natural surroundings. He surveys them, makes decisions, acts. He collects and develops experiences, takes them over from other men, and continues them." Ibid, 150

126. Hannah Arendt, "What was authority," in Carl J. Friedrich, ed., *Authority* (Cambridge, MA: Harvard University Press, 1958).

127. Joyce Little, *The Church and the Culture War* (San Francisco: Ignatius Press, 1995)

128. Genesis, I, 26-28, ii, 7

129. Guardini, *The End of the Modern World*, 133

130. Ibid, 144

131. Ibid, 145

132. Robert K. Greenleaf, *Servant Leadership* (Mahwah, NJ: Paulist Press, 1977), 23-24

133. Ibid, 45

134. Ibid, 61

135. Ken Blanchard and Phil Hodges, *The Servant Leader* (Nashville, TN: J. Countryman, 2003)

136. Little, *The Church and the Culture War*, 30-31

137. Guardini, *The End of the Modern World*, 134

138. G.K. Chesterton, *As I Was Saying* (New York: Dodd, Mead, and Company, 1936), 158

139. Guardini, *The End of the Modern World*, 180

140. Michael C. Jensen and William H. Meckling, "Theory of the Firm: Managerial Behavior, Agency Costs, and Ownership Structure," *Journal of Financial Economics, 3*, 1976.

141. Of this last, the Nobel Prize winning economist Milton Friedman notoriously declared, "the only social responsibility of business is to shareholders." To think otherwise is communism or is at least "taxation without representation." Milton Friedman, "The social responsibility of business is to increase its profits." *New York Times Magazine*, 09/13/1970.

142. See Charles Dickens, *A Christmas Carol* (Clayton, DL: Prestwick House, 2005); Sinclair Lewis, *Babbitt* (San Diego, CA: Harcourt, Brace, Jovanovich, 1922).

143. See Bryan Burrough and John Helyar, *Barbarians at the Gate* (New York: Harper and Row, 1990); Bethany McLean and Peter Elkind, *The Smartest Guys in the Room* (New York: Penguin, 2003).

144. Robert Jackall, *Moral Mazes* (New York: Oxford University, 1988); Christopher Lasch, *The Culture of Narcissism* (New York: W.W. Norton, 1979).

145. This point is being made with increasing frequency, especially by the many writing in the Catholic social tradition (e.g., Helen Alford & Michael J. Naughton, "Beyond the Shareholder Model of the Firm." In S.A. Cortright & Michael J. Naughton (eds.), *Rethinking the Purpose of Business*, (Notre Dame, IN: University of Notre Dame Press, 2002), but also by a few writing in the tradition of science (e.g., Sumatra Ghoshal, "Bad Management Theories are Destroying Good Management Practices," *Academy of Management Learning and Education, 4(1)*, 2005, 75-91).

146. See Lloyd Sandelands, *An Anthropological Defense of God* (New Brunswick, NJ: Transaction, 2007).

147. Because our being is beyond our powers of conception and reason, to know it we require a different knowledge, one that arises not from abstract reasoning, but from the trust and love of intimate personal relationships. This knowledge is connatural as opposed to rational. It is not of the mind alone but of the ensouled body as well. It originates not as a projection of abstract reasoning but as a bodily trust between mother and child. Thus, in "making a life" we come to a startling truth that we have "known all along"—that our business in the world rests not only upon the powers of reason given to us by God our Father, but also and more immediately upon the intimacy and trust we learned from our human mothers . The truth upon which all abstract truths are founded is personal and material. This is the truth of our mothers; an image of the first of all human truths, Jesus Christ. Our being in God is not abstract, but incarnate.

148. John Paul II, *Fides et Ratio*, 14.

149. Ibid, 1

150. Jean-Yves Calvez and Michael J. Naughton, "Catholic Social Teaching and the Purpose of the Business Organization." In S.A. Cortright and Michael J. Naughton (eds.) *Rethinking the Purpose of Business* (Notre Dame, IN: University of Notre Dame Press, 2002), p. 10.

151. John Paul II, *Centesimus Annus*, 41.

152. Ibid, 41. According to John Paul II, "if economic life is absolutized—for example to focus narrowly upon shareholder wealth—the reason is not to find in the eco-

nomic system itself, but in the fact that the socio-cultural system diminishes the ethical and religious dimenion to leave only this secondary value."

153. Ibid

154. Calvez and Naughton, p. 10.

155. John Paul II, *Centesimus Annus*, 41.

156. John Paul II, *Centesimus Annus*, 35.

157. This phrase and that of this section borrows from C.S. Lewis who penned a book of this title.

158. John Paul II, *Centesimus Annus*, 55

159. Ibid, 55

160. *Compendium of the Social Doctrine of the Church* (Vatican: Pontifical Council for Justice and Peace, 2004), 71.

161. Ibid, 73

162. Pastoral Constitution of the Church in the Modern World, *Gaudium et Spes*, Church Council of Vatican II, 1965, #64, 37

163. *Compendium of the Social Doctrine of the Church*, 75

164. Calvez and Naughton, pp. 10-11.

165. *Compendium of the Social Doctrine of the Church*, 81

166. Calvez and Naughton, p. 8.

167. *Gaudium et Spes*, #67, 39

168. Ibid, 39

169. *Compendium of the Social Doctrine of the Church*, 83

170. *Gaudium et Spes*, #68, 39

171. *Compendium of the Social Doctrine of the Church*, 84

172. Thomas Hobbes, *Leviathan* (Indianapolis, IN: Bobbs-Merrill, 1958); Emile Durkheim, *The Division of Labor in Society* (New York: Macmillan, 1933).

173. *Compendium of the Social Doctrine of the Church*, 88

174. Kenneth Arrow, "Methodological individualism and social knowledge," *American Economic Association Papers and Proceedings*, May 1-9, 1994.

175. Ibid, 91

176. *Catechism of the Catholic Church*, 1723.

177. For an exposition of play in the making of human society, see Johan Huizinga, *Homo Ludens* (Boston: Beacon Press, 1950).

178. See Lloyd Sandelands, *Thinking about Social Life* (Lanham, MD: University Press of America, 2003).

179. Michael Novak, *Business as a Calling* (New York: The Free Press, 1996)

180. Ibid, 120

181. Ibid, 123

182. Ibid, 126

183. Ibid, 127

184. Ibid, 131

185. Ibid, 131-2

186. Mary Parker Follett, in Henry C. Metcalf & L. Urwick, eds., *Dynamic Administration: The collected papers of Mary Parker Follett.* (New York: Harper & Brothers, 1942), p. 168

187. Charles Dickens, *A Christmas Carol* (Clayton, DL: Prestwick-House, 2005), 24.

188. Gallup Poll, 12-14-2006

189. C.S. Lewis, *The Business of Heaven* (San Diego: Harcourt, 1984)

190. See Michael Novak, *Business as a Calling* (New York: Free Press, 1996) and D.W. Bakke, *Joy at Work* (Seattle: PVG, 2005).

191. G.E.M. Anscombe, *Human Life, Action, and Ethics*, ed. M. Geach & L Gormally (Charlottesville, VA: Imprint Academic, 2005).

192. See Johan Huizinga, *Homo Ludens* (Boston: Beacon, 1950).

193. See, e.g., Jacques Maritain, *The Person and the Common Good*, trans. J.J. Fitzberald (Notre Dame, IN: Notre Dame Press, 1947).

194. Joyce Little, *The Church and the Culture War* (San Francisco: Harper, 1995).

195. See Lloyd Sandelands, *Male and Female in Social Life* (New Brunswick, NJ: Transaction, 2001).

196. Leslie Brothers, *Friday's Footprint: How Society Shapes the Mind* (New York: Oxford, 1997).

197. Man's twofold creative mind confirms that he/she is a different order of being than animals. Whereas the bodily life of an animal can be divided between its individual organism and the group organism (e.g., colony, flock, school, troop), the creative life of man involves and transcends both. Man's person and society are uniquely integrated in his/her subsistent immaterial being in God. See Lloyd E. Sandelands, *An Anthropological Defense of* God (New Brunswick, NJ: Transaction, 2007).

198. Timothy Fort, "Business as a mediating institution," In S.A. Cortright and M.J. Naughton, *Rethinking the Purpose of Business* (Notre Dame, IN: Notre Dame University, 2002).

199. Saint Augustine, *Confessions* (New York: Knopf, 2001).

200. Dickens, *A Christmas Carol*, 12.

201. See for example, Gerald Davis, *Managed by the Market* (New York: Oxford University Press)

202. Max Weber, *The Protestant Ethic and the Spirit of Capitalism*, trans. T. Parsons (New York: Scribner, 1930).

203. Christopher Lasch, *The Culture of Narcissism* (New York: Norton, 1979).

204. Robert Jackall, "Moral Mazes: Bureaucracy and Managerial Work," *Harvard Business Review*, Sept-Oct, 1983: 1-13, 13).

205. The Wharton School of the University of Pennsylvania, America's first business school, awarded diplomas in accountancy in 1884. The Tuck School at Dartmouth College awarded MBAs to five students in 1901.

206. Jeffrey Pfeffer and Caroline Fong, "The End of Business School? Less Success than Meets the Eye," *Academy of management Learning and Education*, 1(1), 2002: 1-24.

207. It is generally agreed that the impetus for this conversion was a study report on business education commissioned by the Ford Foundation and Carnegie Council. The report by Gordon & Howell criticized American business education for being a collection of trade schools lacking a strong scientific foundation. See R. Gordon & J. Howell, *Higher Education for Business* (New York: Columbia University, 1959).

208. Taken from university website; URL withheld to protect anonymity.

209. Contrast the phrase "human resources management" used today to the older phrase "personnel administration"' employed in the 1950's before business schools embraced science and before the rapid rise of business education in the United States. "Personnel administration" conjures a rather different picture of business, one concerned more with ministering (administration) to persons (personnel) and less with manipulating resources for a purpose. The moral tale of business education is epitomized in its words.

210. Jeffrey Pfeffer and Caroline Fong, "The End of Business Schools," 1.

211. W.G. Bennis and J. O'Toole, "How Business Schools Lost Their Way," *Harvard Business Review*, May, 2005: 94-104, 96.

212. Ibid, 98

213. Ibid, 101

214. Ibid, 104

215. Sumatra Ghoshal, "Bad Management Theories are Destroying Good Management Practices," *Academy of Management Learning and Education*, 4(1), 2005: 75-91, 76.

216. Ibid, 79.

217. Others, of a less charitable bent, refuse to give business schools even this much credit. Business education, they suppose, is not about real expertise, but about a university-sanctioned claim to expertise that justifies the outsized salaries and benefits of business managers. See Alasdair MacIntyre, *After Virtue,* 2e (South Bend, IN: Notre Dame Press, 1984). According to MacIntyre:

> The concept of managerial effectiveness is … a contemporary moral fiction and perhaps the most important of them all. … Belief in managerial expertise is … the illusion of a power not ourselves that claims to make for righteousness. Hence the manager as *character* is other than he at first sight seems to be: the social world of everyday hard-headed practical pragmatic no-nonsense realism which is the environment of management is one which depends for its sustained existence on the systematic perpetuation of misunderstanding and of belief in fictions. The fetishism of commodities has been supplemented by another just as important fetishism, that of bureaucratic skills. For it follows from my whole argument that the realm of managerial expertise is one in which what purport to be objectively-grounded claims function in fact as expressions of arbitrary, but disguised, will and preference (106-107).

218. Dickens, *A Christmas Carol,* 37.

219. MacIntyre, *After Virtue, 2e.*

220. Ibid

221. Milton Friedman, "The Social Responsibility of Business is to Increase Profits," *New York Times Magazine*, 13, 1970: 32-33, 122, 124, 126.

222. Edward Freeman, *Strategic Management: A Stakeholder Approach* (Boston: Pittman, 1984).

223. Joshua Margolis and James Walsh, "Misery Loves Companies: Rethinking Social Initiatives by Business," *Administrative Science Quarterly*, 48, 2003: 265-305.

224. Suggesting this alternative world, see N. Gandal, S. Roccas, I. Sagiv, and A. Wrzesniewski, "Personal value priorities of economists," *Human Relations*, 58(10), 2005: 1227-1252. The authors compared the values of students majoring in economics and students majoring in other fields. Students of economics put more stock in self-enhancement values such as social power, wealth, authority and public image, and less stock in universalism values such as equality, wisdom, social justice, and protection of the environment. See also J. Jordan, "What we don't notice can hurt us (and others): An examination of the cognitive mechanisms behind moral awareness in business," Unpublished manuscript, Tuck School of Business, Dartmouth College, 2007, who compared the economic thinking of business practitioners and non-business practitioners to find that awareness of strategy-related issues came at the expense of awareness of moral-related issues.

225. G.K. Chesterton, *Orthodoxy* (New York: Image Books, 1908), 24.

226. Ibid, 13

227. Lewis, *The Business of Heaven*, 183.
228. Charles Handy, "What's a Business for?" *Harvard Business Review*, 12, Dec., 2002: pp.
229. John Rawls, *A Theory of Justice* (Cambridge, MA: Belknap, 1971).
230. E.g., Josef Ratzinger, "Truth and Freedom," *Communio: International Catholic Review*, Spring, 1996.
231. Dickens, *A Christmas Carol*, 73.
232. Chesterton, *Orthodoxy*, 16.
233. Owen Barfield, *The Rediscovery of Meaning and Other Essays* (Wesleyan, CT: Wesleyan, 1977).
234. Reinhold Niebuhr, *The Nature and Destiny of Man* (New York: Scribner, 1941). According to Neibuhr, human life is distinguished from animal life by its qualified participation in creation. Human existence interferes with the established forms of nature, breaks the forms of nature, and creates new configurations of vitality. This, he argues, is the basis of human history with its progressive alteration of forms, in contrast to nature which knows no history but only endless repetition within the limits of its forms. Man's existential dilemma, according to Niebuhr, is that he cannot solve the problem of his own creativity on his own, but must look to God for limits and direction.
235. Roman Guardini, *The End of the Modern World* (Wilmington, DL: ISI Books, 1998), 209.
236. Ibid, 209.
237. C.S. Lewis, *The Weight of Glory* (San Francisco, Harper, 2001).
238. Niebuhr, *Nature and Destiny*, 179.
239. See e.g., Andrew Delbanco, *The Death of Satan* (New York: Farrar, Straus, and Giroux, 1995).
240. Dickens, *A Christmas Carol*, 14.
241. *Compendium of the Social Doctrine of the Church* (Vatican: Pontifical Council for Justice and Peace, 2004), 71.
242. Ibid, 73
243. Ibid, 75
244. Ibid, 81
245. Ibid, 83
246. Ibid, 84
247. Ibid, 88
248. Ibid, 91
249. Dickens, *A Christmas Carol*, 80.
250. Owen Barfield, *The Rediscovery of Meaning and Other Essays* (Middletown, CT: Wesleyan, 1977)
251. Ibid, 147
252. Walker Percy, *Lost in the Cosmos* (New York: Picador, 1983)
253. According Barfield, *op cit*, 150: "...we live in that abrupt gap between matter and spirit; we exist by virtue of it as autonomous, self-conscious individual spirits, as free beings. Often, in addition, it makes us feel lamentably isolated. But because our freedom and responsibility depend on it, any way that involves disregarding the gap, or pretending it is not there, is a way we take at our peril."
254. Owen Barfield, *Saving the Appearances* (Middletown, CT: Wesleyan University Press, 1965)
255. C.S. Lewis, *A Mind Awake* (Clyde Kilby, ed.) (San Diego: Harvest, 1968), 211

256. Lloyd E. Sandelands, *An Anthropological Defense of God* (New Brunswick, NJ: Transaction, 2007)

257. G.K. Chesterton, *Everlasting Man*, p.?

258. The *Compendium of the Social Doctrine of the Church* (Washington, D.C.: U.S. Conference of Catholic Bishops), p. 115, continues: The wonder of the mystery of man's grandeur makes the psalmist exclaim: "What is man that you are mindful of him, and the son of man that you care for him? Yet you have made him little less than god, and crown him with glory and honor. You have given him dominion over the works of your hands; you have put all things under his feet."

259. John Paul II, In Gary Atkinson, Robert G. Kennedy, & Michael Naughton (eds.), *Dignity of Work: John Paul II Speaks to Managers and Workers* (Lanham, MD: University Press of America, 1995), p. 23.

260. *Compendium of the Social Doctrine of the Church*, 118

261. Ibid, 118

262. Ibid, 21

263. Henry C. Metcalf & L Urwick, Eds., *Dynamic Administration: The Collected Papers of Mary Parker Follett* (New York: Harper & Brothers, 1942), p. 268.

264. Dennis Bakke, *Joy at Work* (Seattle, WA: PVG, 2005), 72

265. Ibid, 18

266. Ibid, 98

267. Ibid, 94-95

268. Ibid, 95

269. Ibid, 139

270. Richard J. Hackman & Gregory Oldham, "Motivation through the design of work: Test of a theory." *Organizational Behavior & Human Performance, 16*(2), 1976, 250–280.

271. Adam Grant, "The significance of task significance: Job performance effects, relational mechanisms, and boundary conditions." *Journal of Applied Psychology, 93, 2008*: 108-124

272. Victor Vroom, *Work Motivation* (New York: John Wiley, 1964)

273. Ernest Becker, *The Birth and Death of Meaning* (New York: Free Press, 1971); Thomas Peters & R.H. Waterman, *In Search of Excellence* (New York: Harper & Row, 1980)

274. http://johncbogle.com/wordpress/wp-content/uploads/2007/05/Georgetown_2007.pdf

275. John M. Czarnetzky, "A Catholic theory of corporate law." *The Catholic Social Science Review, 12*, 2007, 69-82

276. Ibid, 73

277. *Compendium of the Social Doctrine of the Church*, 142

278. Guardini, *The Spirit of the Liturgy*, 13

279. Cited in Robert Fastiggi, "The contributions of Antonio Rosmini (1797-1855) to Catholic social thought." *The Catholic Social Science Review, 12*, 2007, p. 150.

Bibliography

Alford, Helen & Naughton, Michael J. 2002. "Beyond the shareholder model of the firm." In S.A. Cortright & Michael J. Naughton (eds.). *Rethinking the purpose of business.* Notre Dame, IN: University of Notre Dame.

Anscombe, G.E.M. 2005. In M. Geach and L. Gormally (eds.). *Human life, action and ethics.* Charlottesville, VA: Imprint Academic.

Arendt, Hannah 1958. "What was authority?" In Carl J. Friedrich, ed. *Authority.* Cambridge, MA: Harvard.

Arrow, K. 1994. "Methodological individualism and social knowledge," *American Economic Association Papers and Proceedings,* May 1-9.

Argyris, Chris 1957. *Personality and organization.* New York: Harper & Row.

Augustine, Saint 2001. *The confessions.* New York: Alfred A. Knopf.

Bailie, G. 2004. "The subject of Gaudium et Spes: Reclaiming a Christocentric anthropology of the human person." www.stthomas.edu/cathstudies/

Bakke, Dennis W. 2005. *Joy at work.* Seattle, WA: PVG.

Barber, Benjamin 2007. *Consumed.* New York: Norton.

Barfield, Owen 1965. *Saving the appearances.* Wesleyan, CT: Wesleyan Press.

Barfield, Owen 1977. *The rediscovery of meaning and other essays.* Wesleyan, CT: Wesleyan Press.

Becker, Ernest 1971. *The birth and death of meaning.* New York: Free Press.

Bennis, Warren G. & Nanus, Burt 1985. *Leaders: The strategies for taking charge.* New York: Harper & Row.

Bennis, Warren G. & O'Toole, J. 2005. "How business schools lost their way." *Harvard Business Review*, May, 96, 94-104.

Blanchard, Ken & Hodges, Phil 2003. *The servant leader.* Nashville, TN: J. Countryman.

Brothers, Leslie 1997. *Friday's footprint: How society shapes the mind.* New York: Oxford.

Buber, Martin 1958. *I and thou.* New York: Charles Scribner's Sons

Budziszewski, J. 2004. *What we can't not know.* Dallas, TX: Spence

Burrough, Bryan & Helyar, J. 1990. *Barbarians at the gate.* New York: Harper & Row.

Calvez, Jean-Yves & Naughton, Michael J. 2002. "Catholic social teaching and the purpose of the business organization." In S.A. Cortright and M.J. Naugton (eds.) *Rethinking the purpose of business.* Notre Dame, IN: University of Notre Dame.

Carnetzky, John M. 2007. "A Catholic theory of corporate law." *The Catholic Social Science Review, 12*: 69-82.

Catechism of the Catholic Church, 1995. New York: Doubleday.

Chesterton, G.K. 1908. *Orthodoxy.* New York: Image Books.

Chesterton, G.K. 1936. *As I was saying.* New York: Dodd, Mead, and Company.

Chesterton, G.K. 1974. *The everlasting man.* Westport, CT: Greenwood Press.

Cialdini, Robert 2001. "Harnessing the science of persuasion." *Harvard Business Review*, October, 74.

Compendium of the social doctrine of the Church, 2004. Vatican: Pontifical Council for Justice and Peace.

Davis, Gerald F. 2009. *Managed by the Market.* New York: Oxford University Press.

Delbanco, Andrew 1995. *The death of Satan.* New York: Farrar, Straus & Giroux.

Dickens, Charles 2005. *A Christmas carol.* Clayton, DL: Prestwick House.
Durkheim, Emile 1933. *The division of labor in society.* New York: Macmillan.
Ehrenreich, Barbara 2006. *Bait and switch.* New York: Owl Books.
Fastiggi, Robert 2007. "The contributions of Antonio Rosmini (1797-1855) to Catholic social thought." *The Catholic Social Science Review, 12.*
Fisher, H.E. 1982. *The sex contract: The evolution of human behavior.* New York: William Morrow.
Follett, Mary Parker 1942. In H.C. Metcalf & L. Urwick (eds). *Dynamic Administration: The collected papers of Mary Parker Follett.* New York: Harper & Brothers.
Fort, Timothy 2002. "Business as a mediating institution." In S. Cortright & M.J. Naughton (eds.). *Rethinking the purpose of business.* Notre Dame, IN: University of Notre Dame.
Frank, Thomas 2000. *One market under God.* New York: Doubleday.
Freeman, Edward 1984. *Strategic management: A stakeholder approach.* Boston: Pittman Press.
French, John & Raven, Bertran 1959. "The bases of social power." In D. Cartwright (ed.), *Studies in social power.* Ann Arbor, MI: University of Michigan.
Friedman, Milton 1970. "The social responsibility of business is to increase its profits." *New York Times Magazine*, September, 13, 1970.
Friedman, Milton & Friedman, Rose 1980. *Free to Choose.* New York: Harcourt, Brace & Jovanovich.
Gandal, N. Roccas, S., Sagiv, L. & Wrzesniewski, A. 2005. "Personal value priorities of economists." *Human Relations, 58(10)*: 1227-1252.
Gaudium et Spes, 1965, Church Council of Vatican II, #64, 37.
Ghoshal, Sumatra 2005. "Bad management theories are destroying good management practices." *Academy of Management Learning and Education, 4(1)*, 75-91.
Gibran, Kahil, 1923. *The prophet.* New York: Knopf.
Gordon, R. & Howell, J. 1959. *Higher education for business.* New York: Columbia University.
Grant, Adam, 2008. "The significance of task significance: Job performance effects, relational mechanisms, and boundary conditions." *Journal of Applied Psychology*, 93: 108-124
Greenleaf, Robert K. 1977. *Servant leadership.* Mahwah, NJ: Paulist Press.
Guardini, Romano 1998. *The end of the modern world.* Wilmington, DL: ISI Books.
Guardini, Romano 1998. *The spirit of the liturgy.* New York: Herder & Herder.
Hackman, Richard J. & Gregory Oldham, 1976. "Motivation through the design of work: Test of a theory." *Organizational Behavior and Human Performance, 16(2)*: 250-280.
Handy, Charles 2002. What's a business for?" *Harvard Business Review*, December.
Heilbronner, Robert 1961. *The worldly philosophers.* New York: Time Inc.
Hobbes, Thomas 1958. *Leviathan.* Indianapolis, IN: Bobbs-Merrill.
Huizinga, Johan 1950. *Homo ludens.* Boston: Beacon Press.
Jackall, Robert 1988. *Moral mazes.* New York: Oxford University.
James, William 1902. *The varieties of religious experience.* New York: Longmans, Greene & Company.
James, William 1963. *Pragmatism and other essays.* New York: Washington Square Books.
Jensen, Michael & Meckling, William H. 1976. "Theory of the firm: Managerial behavior, agency costs, and ownership structure." *Journal of Financial Economics, 3.*
John Paul II. 1981. Encyclical letter: *Laborem Exercens*, www.vatican.va/
John Paul II 1991. Encyclical letter: *Centesimus Annus*, www.vatican.va/

John Paul II 1994. *Crossing the threshold of hope*. London: Knopf.

John Paul II 1995. In Gary Atkinson, Robert G. Kennedy, & Michael Naughton (eds.). *Dignity of work: John Paul II speaks to managers and workers*. Lanham, MD: University Press of America.

John Paul II 1996. Apostolic exhortation: *Familaris Consortio*, www.vatican.va/

John Paul II 1998. Encyclical letter: *Fides et Ratio*, www.vatican.va/

Jones, Edward D. 1918. *The administration of industrial enterprises*. New York: Longmans, Greene & Company.

Kass, Leon R. 2002. *Life, liberty, and the defense of dignity*. San Francisco: Encounter.

Langer, Suzanne 1967. *Mind: An essay on human feeling, Vol. 1*. Baltimore, MD: Johns Hopkins Press.

Lasch, Christopher 1979. *The culture of narcissism*. New York: Norton.

Lewis, C.S. 1968. *A mind awake*. (Clyde Kilby, ed.). San Diego, CA: Harvest.

Lewis, C.S. 1984. *The business of heaven*. San Diego, CA: Harcourt.

Lewis. C.S. 2001. *The weight of glory*. San Francisco: Harper.

Lewis, C.S. 2001. *The abolition of man*. San Francisco: Harper.

Lewis, Sinclair 1922. *Babbitt*. San Diego, CA: Harcourt, Brace, Jovanovich.

Little, Joyce 1995. *The Church and the culture war*. San Francisco: Ignatius Press.

MacIntyre, Alasdair 1984. *After virtue, 2e*. Notre Dame, IN: University of Notre Dame.

Mannes, Marya 1964. *But will it sell?* Philadelphia: Lippincott.

March, James G. & Simon, Herbert H. 1958. *Organizations*. New York: Wiley.

Margolis, Joshua & Walsh, James P. 2003. "Misery loves companies: Rethinking social initiatives by business. *Administrative Science Quarterly, 48*: 265-305.

Maritan, Jacques 1947. *The person and the common good*. Trans. J.J. Fitzgerald. Notre Dame, IN: University of Notre Dame.

Mayo, Elton 1945. *Problems of industrial civilization*. Boston: Harvard.

McGregor, Douglas 1960. *The human side of enterprise*. New York: McGraw-Hill.

McLean, Bethany & Elkind, Peter 2003. *The smartest guys in the room*. New York: Penguin.

Mead, Margaret 1949. *Male and female*. New York: Morrow.

Niebuhr, Reinhold 1941. *The nature and destiny of man*. New York: Scribner.

Novak, Michael 1996. *Business as a calling*. New York: The Free Press.

Pascal, Blaise 1931. *Thoughts* (selections). London: J.M. Dent.

Percy, Walker 1983. *Lost in the cosmos*. New York: Picador.

Percy, Walker 1991. *Signposts in a strange land*. New York: Picador.

Peters, Thomas & Waterman, Robert H. 1982. *In search of excellence*. New York: Warner Books.

Pfeffer, Jeffrey 1992. *Managing with power*. Boston: Harvard Business School Press.

Pfeffer, Jeffrey & Fong, Caroline 2002. "The end of business school? Less success than meets the eye." *Academy of Management Learning and Education, 1(1)*: 1-24.

Ratzinger, Josef 1990. *Introduction to Christianity*. San Francisco: Ignatius Press.

Ratzinger, Josef 1996. "Truth and freedom." *Communio: International Catholic Review*, Spring.

Rawls, John 1971. *A theory of justice*. Cambridge, MA: Belknap.

Sandelands, Lloyd E. 2001. *Male and female in social life*. New Brunswick, NJ: Transaction.

Sandelands, Lloyd E. 2003. *Thinking about social life*. Lanham, MD: University Press of America.

Sandelands, Lloyd E. 2005. *Man and nature in God*. New Brunswick, NJ: Transaction.

Sandelands, Lloyd E. 2007. *An anthropological defense of God*. New Brunswick, NJ: Transaction.

Scott, W. Richard & Davis, Gerald F. 2007. *Organizations and organizing: Rational, Natural, and Open-systems Perspectives.* New York: Prentice-Hall.

Smuts, Barbara 1985. *Sex and friendship in baboons.* New York: Aldine de Gruyter.

Stern, Karl 1965. *The flight from woman.* New York: Farrar, Strauss & Giroux.

Taylor, Frederick 1911. *The principles of scientific management.* New York: Norton.

Tolstoy, Leo 1997. *A calendar of wisdom.* Trans. By P. Sekirin. New York: Scribner.

Urwick, L. 1943. *The elements of administration.* New York: Harper & Brothers.

Vroom, Victor 1964. *Work motivation.* New York: John Wiley.

Weber, Max 1958. *The protestant ethic and the spirit of capitalism.* New York: Scribner's Sons.

Whitehead, Alfred North 1925. *Science and the modern world.* New York: Macmillan.

Zander, Rosamund S. & Zander, Benjamin 2002. *The art of possibility.* New York: Penguin.

Index

About the Author

Lloyd E. Sandelands teaches business administration and psychology at the University of Michigan in Ann Arbor. His research focuses on the social and spiritual life of business. He is the author of *Feeling and Form in Social Life* (1998, Rowman & Littlefield), *Male and Female in Social Life* (2001, Transaction), *Thinking about Social Life* (2003, University Press of America), *Man and Nature in God* (2005, Transaction), and *An Anthropological Defense of God* (2007, Transaction).